Dombroff On Dombroff

Magic in the Courtroom

By

Mark Dombroff

Austin Brothers Publishing
Fort Worth, TX

Dombroff on Dombroff: Magic in the Courtroom
© 2020 by Mark Dombroff
Published by Austin Brothers Publishing

ISBN: 978-1-7359739-0-6
Library of Congress Number: 2020920758

Printed in the United States

Other Books by Mark Dombroff

- Key Trial Control Tactics (2 volumes)
- Dombroff on Demonstrative Evidence
- Dombroff on Direct and Cross-Examination
- Dombroff on Unfair Tactics
- Trial Objections
- Trial Hearsay
- Federal Trial Evidence
- Premises Security
- Evaluating and Reserving Wrongful Death and Personal Injury Cases
- Expert Witnesses in Civil Trials: Effective Preparation and Presentation
- Discovery
- Litigation Organization and Management: Effective Techniques and Tactics
- Personal Injury Defense Techniques (3 volumes)
- Negligence Litigation Handbook: Federal and State
- Dynamic Closing Arguments

To my parents, Eunice and Ben Dombroff,
both lawyers.
They inspired me to become a lawyer,
and along the way,
endured me becoming a magician.

To my wife, Jan, who has been with me
throughout my journey.

And to my daughter, Jessica, of whom I am
immensely proud.

Acknowledgments

By now, you know the title of this book, *Dombroff on Dombroff: Magic in the Courtroom*. When I wrote the foreword, I wasn't sure what the title would be. As I thought about it, given the fact that I've written things like Dombroff on *Demonstrative Evidence* and *Dombroff on Direct and Cross-Examination*, I started thinking about naming this book *Dombroff on Dombroff*. It's by me about me, but most important, it's for me. As I thought about it further, I decided I wanted to hear someone else's view of that title, since even to me, it sounded sort of arrogant, after all, *Dombroff on Dombroff*.

I spoke to my publisher, Terry Austin, at Austin Brothers Publishing and asked Terry if it sounded sort of arrogant to title it that way. Terry, who has provided invaluable assistance and support throughout this project, wasted no time asking how could it be arrogant when I was, after all, writing a book about myself. He was right. In some respect, the height of arrogance is writing a book about yourself, but I was writing for me. This book will never make the bestseller list and will never be made into a movie, but at least in my mind, it will be a bestseller, and even better than a movie, I lived it.

Chapters

Foreword

When it comes to writing a book, some authors settle on a book title before writing a manuscript even begins. In most cases, a title comes to light at some point in the writing, and the paragraphs and chapters flow together. In my case, I have a complete manuscript in front of me without a title.

I considered two alternatives. One is *Dombroff on Dombroff*, and the other is *Don't Get Even, Get Mad*. There's a history, or should I say a story, behind both options.

Throughout my long career, I've written hundreds and hundreds of articles and given hundreds and hundreds of speeches and presentations. I've also written over a dozen books for trial lawyers. These books covered various aspects of trial practice. My first book consisted of two volumes and was called *Key Trial Control Tactics*. Other books dealt with subjects like direct and cross-examination, demonstrative evidence, unfair tactics, expert witnesses, hearsay evidence, federal rules of evidence, defense techniques, and others. They covered nearly every aspect of trial practice.

Many of the books utilized my name in the title, for example, *Dombroff on Demonstrative Evidence*, or *Dombroff on Direct and Cross-Examination*. The books were based on my personal experience and the things I learned while practicing law myself. They were not just theoretical, and adding my name to the title emphasized the real-life nature of the subject. As I began this book, the title, *Dombroff On Dombroff*, popped into my head as a natural fit.

Given the theme of trial practice, I discovered that writing a book for lawyers was easier, in many respects, than writing this book. All of those previous books were created to convey trial practice techniques and methods I had developed over my career. They were written to help lawyers learn from my expe-

rience. Although this book is certainly for lawyers, the target is much broader. It is not just for lawyers.

Many of the concepts I wrote about in my previous books are also discussed in this book. However, the discussion here is not in terms of how to develop the skill. This book is about the context of the cases where those skills were learned. This is the only book, and indeed, it's the only thing I've ever written for me. Looking back over 50 years, and as I write, it is 50 years of practicing law, I felt that I wanted to write for my benefit, not to teach others. My hope is that others will find my experiences interesting, maybe even instructive.

That is why I thought the title, *Dombroff On Dombroff* might be appropriate. It says it all since it is a book about me and my career.

The other title that came to mind, *Don't Get Even, Get Mad,* needs some explana-tion. My full name, including my middle name, is Mark Andrew Dombroff. You've probably already de-duced that my initials are "MAD." Many law firms have slogans, and the phrase, "Don't get even, get MAD," would make sense for my law firm if we had a slogan. Even though I had my law firm for 20 years, that was nev-er our slogan.

With Mom and Dad

My parents frequently told a story about me as a baby. My mother and father were both lawyers, and when I came along, they obtained a baby carriage. This was back in the day before the style of baby strollers we use now. Many of these baby carriages, or buggies, were elaborate. They had four large wheels with springs and shock absorbers. They were often highly lacquered and elaborate.

A baby's initials were sometimes placed on the side of the carriage, which, in my case, was "MAD." That was always an eye-catcher, and my mother used to tell me that people often commented about a baby with the word "mad" on their carriage. My mother told me she responded that given the fact that she was a lawyer, she expected her son to be a lawyer also and that the letters were more than initials. They were entirely appropriate because she said she could then tell them that when I grew up, the slogan of my law firm would be, "Don't get even; get mad." If you knew my mother, you would believe that story.

As I write these words and fill out the paragraphs, I haven't decided or settled on the title for the book. However, by the time you read these words, you will know my ultimate decision. At least, assuming it's one of these two titles, you will know how I arrived at that conclusion. I thought it would be helpful, maybe interesting, or amusing for you to understand where the title came from. Who knows, it might even turn out to be something entirely different.

I hope you find reading about my experiences as interesting as it was for me to be there and be a part of creating them. Nothing of what I experienced over my professional life was done alone. Over the years, whether at the FAA, the Department of Justice, or the various law firms and lawyers I was privileged to work with, I have been fortunate to work with, encounter, and oppose very talented lawyers. All of them had a significant role to play in the stories you will read. My list includes expert witnesses, judges, juries, clients, and many others who shared in the experiences.

Enjoy!

The Babylift Case

A request to appear before a Federal Judge was not unusual since I was a Director of the Civil Division with the Department of Justice. When one of the Deputy Clerks called requesting my presence, I wasn't surprised or concerned about anything in particular. I was knee-deep in a pretty high-profile case with Federal Judge Louis F. Oberdorfer, and it was his clerk who sent the message.

The next day, I packed up my briefcase and made the short trip to the Federal Courthouse. This was before 9/11, and courthouse security wasn't as meticulous as today, so I walked in and headed upstairs to the Ceremonial Courtroom, where I was scheduled to meet the Judge.

Every Judge has a courtroom assigned strictly for their use, but the Ceremonial Courtroom is much larger than the others. Not only is there more room for spectators, but the bench is enormous—large enough for every sitting Federal Judge in the district. You've probably seen photos of the Supreme Court Justices sitting behind one large bench. That will provide an image of what is in the courtroom I entered, except much larger.

I opened the door of the courtroom, expecting to see people inside. Instead, it was empty, completely empty—no spectators, court officers, or judges on the bench. As I stepped into the courtroom, a door behind the Judge's bench slowly swung open. A U.S. Federal Courthouse Marshal, unmistakable because of his badge, walked through the door and said, "Mr. Dombroff?"

I replied with a simple, "Yes."

"Please come with me."

I walked to the front of the courtroom and followed him through the door. The door led to a conference room that sat directly behind the bench. It's a huge conference room with a massive table. In fact, it's probably the largest conference table I've ever seen, and I've seen many over the years.

There wasn't time to marvel at the size of the room and the table because sitting there waiting for me was every Federal Judge from the United States District Court for the District of Columbia, more than a dozen of them. I didn't take roll to see if everyone was there, but it sure seemed to me that every chair was taken. I had walked into an *en banc* session of the Federal Court in Washington, D.C.

Judge Oberdorfer was there, but the Chief Judge of the district took control of the meeting. At that level, a Chief Judge operates in his/her District like the Chief Justice of the Supreme Court. The judges are all equal, but the Chief Judge has administrative responsibilities and typically oversees the meetings of the court.

Although I wasn't quite sure the purpose of the meeting, it was clear to me early that the judges were not happy. I was basically told that what was happening with the cases in which I was defending the United States was unacceptable to the bench. We were in a situation where the cases were going to

tie up every Judge for at least two years. It was made clear that
they wanted me to settle the cases.

I attempted to explain the problem and why it wasn't that
simple, but it was clear they weren't having it. After some discussion, the Chief Judge said, "You will settle these cases, and
this is how much the United States of America will pay."

He wrote something on a piece of yellow legal paper,
folded it over, and slid it across the table to me. When it made
its way across the massive desk, I picked it up, opened it, and
all I saw was a number—nothing else, just a number. I don't
remember the number, but that's all it was, a number, nothing
else.

After looking it over, I said, "Your Honors, even if I wanted to settle this case today, and even if I wanted to say yes
to this, I have no authorization to do so. This number would
have to go to the Deputy Attorney General and probably the
Attorney General."

Their response was essentially, "Do whatever you have to
do, but get these cases resolved!"

This situation began with a plane crash in Vietnam.

As the Vietnam War drew rapidly to a conclusion in 1975,
more than 3,000 orphaned infants and young children were
evacuated from South Vietnam, in addition to the more than
100,000 refugees. Thousands of the children were airlifted to
families around the world waiting to adopt them.

The plan was to evacuate the children on 30 planned
flights aboard military aircraft, including the monstrous C-5A
Galaxy aircraft operated by the Air Force. Numerous service

organizations were involved in recruiting families and placing orphans, more than 2,500 to the States.

On April 4, 1975, as part of *Operation Babylift*, an Air Force C-5A departed the airport in Saigon late in the afternoon. Only 12 minutes into the flight, the rear cargo door latch failed, allowing the ramp used for loading the aircraft to fly open. This meant the plane was depressurized, and the hydraulic cables that controlled the tail of the aircraft were cut.

Wrestling with the controls, the pilots were able to turn the plane around and return toward the airport. Realizing they were not going to make it to the runway, the pilots were able to guide the plane into a rice paddy where it skipped and bounced until finally coming to a sudden stop as it plowed into a dyke. The plane broke apart and burst into flames. The final tally revealed 138 deaths, including 78 children, with many more injured.

The military conducted an investigation. Since the North Vietnamese were moving toward Saigon at that time, the investigators were helicoptered out at night to keep them safe. The result of the investigation was litigation in Federal Court in Washington D.C., filed by an organization called *Friends for all Children*. They represented all the orphans who had been brought to the United States for the purpose of being adopted. This group represented dozens of them.

Some of the adopted children died in the crash, but most survived. The survivors had injuries of all kinds ranging from physical ones that could be seen, internal ones that were diagnosed, and others claiming the likelihood of future problems caused by hypoxia suffered when the plane lost oxygen. Many

of these injuries were not visually apparent but only asserted as
a possibility in the future.

Lawsuits were filed against Lockheed, the designer,
and manufacturer of the C-5A, as well as the United States
Government for negligence in connection with the operation
and maintenance of the aircraft by the Air Force. These suits
were filed in the Federal District Court in Washington D.C., and
a Guardian ad litem was appointed to represent the interests of
the children. Virtually all of them already had adoptive parents
waiting for them to arrive in the U.S., but in most instances, the
adoptions were awaiting finalization.

The lawsuits were heavily contested, and they were all
consolidated before Judge Louis Oberdorfer in Washington.
The process of discovery depositions and document production went on for a very long time, a number of years. It continued, even after I became the Director in 1980, five years after the
accident.

Periodically, I, along with two other lawyers who worked
for me at Justice, had to appear in court for hearings with Judge
Oberdorfer. It became clear to me very early that the Judge was
very frustrated with the case. The number of cases, close to 100,
was challenging. He couldn't figure out how to try them in a
way that wouldn't take forever. He decided to pick out some
bell-weather cases—a severe injury case, a non-physical injury
case, a case with asserted brain damage, and a death case. He
would then use those cases as benchmark cases for all the others
and hope that it resulted in settlements of the rest of the cases.

We objected to that approach, based on our position that
causation every one of the children was different. Lockheed

was even more vehemently opposed, but the Judge went ahead with his plan.

As soon as verdicts came in, appeals were taken to the Court of Appeals. At that point, they were reversed, and the Appeals Court affirmed that it could not be done that way because causation was, as both Lockheed and the United States had argued, different in every single case. Every person, every child, and every plaintiff was different, and the defendants had the right to challenge causation, subject to physical examinations, based on where they were sitting on the plane, and other factors. The grand scheme the Judge had devised fell apart. Every case had to go to trial.

All the cases were sent back to Judge Oberdorfer, and each would have to be tried separately. The ones that had already been tried lasted two or three weeks each. With dozens of these cases requiring jury trials, we were in a situation where one Judge would spend the rest of his/her career with only these cases. Judge Oberdorfer was not pleased with that scenario—neither was the Chief Judge.

Both Lockheed and the Government, which I represented, tried to settle the cases, but the plaintiffs were unwilling. They didn't think the money offered was enough. As I think back over the years, I don't believe that Judge Oberdorfer provided any particular assistance to the parties achieving settlement. He did little to encourage plaintiffs to settle. Frankly, I think the case was bigger than his ability to manage them, and that it was pretty much out of control.

The most challenging problem was the infants, many of them just a few months old at the time of the accident. The Plaintiffs pushed the idea that they suffered brain damage due

to hypoxia. There was no way to prove or disprove that assertion. We were looking years down the road, so how were we
supposed to compensate based on the notion they may have
brain damage. If they have problems for the rest of their life,
you were talking about vast amounts of money with no ability
to project what that would be, much less whether it would even
occur.

After all that, Judge Oberdorfer now had a docket full of
cases, and the Court of Appeals has already told him he can't
do what he had planned on doing. I'm not exactly sure how
it happened, but Judge Oberdorfer then managed to distribute
the cases to every sitting judge on the D.C. bench. So, every sitting Federal Judge in Washington ended up with five or six cases they would have to try, each of them requiring at least three
to five weeks.

Basically, what Judge Oberdorfer did was take a judi-
cial management problem that he had created and decided to
share with will all his colleagues on the bench. I would love to
have been a fly on the wall as some of these judges found out
what was happening. That was the situation when I received
the phone call to report to the Ceremonial Courtroom and see
Judge Oberdorfer.

I'll never forget walking into that conference room and seeing all those judges. When the meeting concluded, I went back
to the Department and conferred with the Assistant Attorney
General. I described everything that had transpired, and he was
as surprised as I was.

Ultimately, all the cases got settled, not individually, but
rather by setting up a Medical Trust funded by Lockheed and
the United States. We didn't write a check to the plaintiffs.

Instead, we established a trust fund to be available to monitor the medical condition of the children as they grew older. This money was used to pay medical expenses, if any, with the unused funds reverting back to Lockheed and the United States at the termination of the trust.

In addition to the unusual nature of the accident, the uniqueness of the passengers on board, all of them infants, made it more than interesting. I've handled numerous other plane crashes in my career and never had the experience of the court effectively "ordering" the United States Department of Justice to get a case settled. From the court's perspective, the alternative was for the entire court to come to a grinding halt.

Those children and infants are now in their 40s. I have learned over the years that in the aviation area that passengers from crashes and/or their families tend to stay in touch, so it would not surprise me to learn these children, now adults, have created some kind of affinity group. An explosive collective experience creates a powerful attraction to others who shared the experience.

Growing Up

Erle Stanley Gardner wrote nearly 100 detective and mystery novels that each sold a million copies. Even if you haven't read any of his books, you're probably familiar with the lawyer who was central to most of his stories—*Perry Mason*. The best-selling books were turned into a television series starring Raymond Burr as the relentless lawyer. Many Saturday nights, we gathered around the black and white television, mesmerized as we saw Mason coax a witness on the stand to confess to a crime or expose a valuable piece of evidence. I was hooked.

It's not surprising that I've been a lawyer for 50 years because both of my parents were lawyers. Both attended St. John's University Law School in New York. At the time, it was not nearly as common as it is today for women to be lawyers. After graduating, Mom became an Assistant Corporation Counsel for the City of New York.

My mom graduating from law school

15

My father went to the service before law school and served in the military during World War II. For as long as I can remember, he was a sole practitioner and shared the rent and space with other sole practitioners. Each lawyer had their desk and small working space. There came a point when Dad left the law and went to work in the business world. Ultimately, he became the President of Willoughby's in New York. At the time, it was the world's largest retailer of cameras. That's what he did for most of my growing up years. The company, or at least the name, is still in business today, selling cameras.

Stored away in my library are some of his briefs from the time when my Dad was still in private practice. I remember reading them and coming across some quotes in appellate briefs from lower courts where an appeal had been taken from the trial court. They cited and discussed my Dad's oral arguments. All I ever knew growing up was lawyers, lawyers, lawyers.

On my mother's side, my grandfather was a doctor. He was a traditional M.D., the kind who made house calls. He and my grandmother lived in Manhattan. When I stayed over at their apartment, he would leave in the middle of the night to make a house call; that was truly the "old days."

My grandmother was a unique woman. She was an opera singer, a collector of Asian art, and a poet. In fact,

My Dad

a collection of her poetry and papers is currently housed at Syracuse University.

I was born in 1947 when it was uncommon for a woman to keep working after having kids. Mom never practiced law after I was born, that I'm aware of. Five years after my arrival, my younger brother came along. As we both got older, Mom started looking for something to do and went back to college. Although she already had a law degree, she earned enough credits to obtain a teaching license. By this time, we had moved to Long Island, and she got a job teaching history in high school, a profession she maintained for 30 or more years until she retired.

There came a time, probably in his late 50s or early 60s, when my father began to manifest memory loss. Although he was ultimately diagnosed with

My Grandmother

Alzheimer's, he died in his early 60s following an auto accident. My mother lived into her 80s.

Without giving it much thought, I always assumed I would be a lawyer. It wasn't a conscious career decision, but my fascination with *Perry Mason* stayed with me. The thing I talk about in speeches is that in many respects, that television show, and its progeny, ruined American juries for lawyers. By watching somebody like *Perry Mason*, as well as the law practiced on

My Mother - the biker!!!

most of the TV other shows, people have come to expect that in an hour or two hours, the crime gets committed, the perpetrator gets caught, he/she gets tried, and justice is handed out. It's all accomplished within an hour or two hours, including commercials.

The offshoot of that is that many, maybe most, people come to court as jurors, and their only exposure to lawyers or trials is from television or movies, or these days Netflix. They expect they will not only decide guilt or innocence, but if the defendant is not guilty, then who is? They think the defense lawyer will explain it all to them if it's a criminal case. If it's a civil case, they expect to discover if the defendant wasn't responsible, then who is to blame? They need an alternate explanation.

I don't blame them for having this need to unmask the wrongdoer. Human nature suggests the necessity to hold someone responsible. However, our system is not designed to work that way. In our system, there's a presumption of innocence on the criminal side and a presumption of no wrongdoing on the civil side. The prosecutor in the criminal case has to prove their case beyond a reasonable doubt. This doesn't mean beyond any doubt but a reasonable doubt, and on the civil side, the plaintiff has to prove their case by a preponderance of the evidence.

Even though the judge instructs the jury about the burden of proof, the fact of the matter is that, as a lawyer, I'm always going to come up with an alternative theory or theories of who is to be blamed. That's something I had to learn. It's a practical lesson that goes back to when I was growing up watching Raymond Burr's *Perry Mason*.

Although they had both been lawyers, my parents were patient for me to decide for myself. I chose to go to law school only after I had been accepted. I had to decide during my final year of college if I wanted law school or business graduate school. I chose law school, but I was well into my first year when I finally concluded it was the right decision for me.

MARK DOMBROFF
FOX ROTHSCHILD

Even before I was thinking about the law, or even knew my parents were lawyers, far back as age six or seven, I became absolutely enamored with magicians and magic. It became my hobby. I was the stereotypical annoying kid who constantly wanted to show everyone, my mother, in particular, a magic trick. It has stuck with me my entire life.

My grandfather, the doctor, supported my magic passion. When I went into New York City to visit them, he always took me to one of the magic shops. One of the first magic books I ever had was volume 1 of a set called *Greater Magic*, and my grandfather inscribed it for me for my eighth birthday. I treasure it today.

Some of the magic in my office

I've performed magic in front of audiences at the World's Fair in New York in the 1960s to corporate occasions and even birthday parties—the typical sort of birthday party where magicians have rabbits. My whole life, my motto has been "have magic, will travel." I've also collected magic apparatus, books, and paraphernalia for as long as I remember. I have a gigantic collection. My office is filled with magic stuff, and I'm beginning to consider if it might be time to start auctioning some things. There is even a magic theater at my house with all the collections arranged around the room and a magic library for my book collection.

Being passionate about cars is another part of my life, but until I was able to afford it, it was sorely undeveloped. Even though my father was a lawyer/business executive and mother, a lawyer, and a teacher, I grew up quite middle class. Our home was a garden apartment in Queens. When I was in the seventh grade, we moved to Oceanside, Long Island, a middle-class community where we had a tract home. We did fine, but I never lived with luxury growing up.

Consequently, I was never able to develop my interest in cars until my financial situation changed and made it possible. I'm not a high-value collector of cars, but I do have an interest in specific vehicles. One that always seemed unreachable to me when I was growing up was a Jaguar XKE. I always saw it as the ultimate car, but it only existed on television or in commercials.

When finally able, I purchased a bright red 1963 Jaguar XKE Roadster with wire wheels and black leather. I bought it on eBay, sight unseen, and had it shipped to my house in Virginia. There it sat in my garage for a couple of years until I had it restored. It's beautiful, to the point I was inspired to purchase another—a 1964 Jaguar XKE Coupe, the sister car to my 1963. I do not claim to be a collector. Perhaps "accumulator" is a more accurate term. I don't buy and sell; I accumulate.

From Oceanside High School, I went to American University, a private school in Washington D.C. Until then, I had never been away from home other than taking the train from Long Island to visit my grandparents. My father and I took the train to visit the campus in Washington, and I immediately fell in love with the campus and the city.

Certainly, I didn't realize it at the time, but Washington D.C. and its suburbs became my home for the rest of my life. It all began with college, and like many others, I can say that those four years were among the best years of my life. I joined a fraternity and made friends, having remained friends with most of my fraternity brothers for the past 50 years.

Magic... Magic... Magic

Magic! Nothing has served my professional career as well as learning magic as a kid. It goes back to when I was only six years old. I don't recall the specific moment that ignited my interest in magic, but something captured my attention, and I never, to this day, let go. Most young magicians outgrow the interest quickly, but I continued to grow, year after year.

My mother gave me an old makeup case with various fitted sections and compartments to keep all the items from my tricks. It was slightly larger than a briefcase, and I made good use of that case for a long time. I was the perennial "let me show you a trick" kid to my parents and grandparents. As I grew, my interest in magic also continued to grow. Any money that I made from shoveling snow or a paper route was saved for a trip on the Long Island Railroad into New York, where I visited the magic shop.

The first magic shop I ever visited, more than 65 years ago was a place called "Circle Magic." It was in a big arcade in the heart of Manhattan at Times Square. My grandfather took me there, and still, to this day, I have the magic tricks he bought for me at that store. The tricks were "The Color Vision Cube, "A

Royal Magic Penetration Frame," and a "Square Circle," a silk handkerchief production.

As I got more and more involved in magic, my shows became more and more elaborate. I put on shows in our garage for the neighborhood kids. I learned about other magic shops in New York, including "Lou Tannen's." It was not just a magic shop; it was a magical place. It was on the 12th floor of what was the Wurlitzer Building near the New York Public Library. It's the oldest operating magic store in New York City, founded in 1925. Every magician in America knows of Lou Tannen's.

It wasn't a place for anyone to simply walk in from the street. You had to be a magician even to know it was there. I always came home from my trips to Tannens with a treasure trove of new tricks. I still remember all the magicians in Suite 1207 at 120 W. 42nd Street showing magic tricks to one another with Lou Tannen and other demonstrators behind the counter showing the latest wares.

I became passionate about magic and magicians. I watched everything I could find on TV, including the Festival of Magic in 1957. It was the time of black and white television, at least that's what we had, but I loved the show. Magic had my attention—I loved learning it, watching it, reading about it, and probably most of all, performing it. Unknowingly at the time, it was building my confidence. It made me comfortable speaking and performing in front of my friends and even adults. That's a strength I've carried and built upon throughout my professional career as a lawyer.

At the time, I was unaware that the people walking through the doors at that 12trh story Tannen's Magic shop were the legends of the magic world. They would mean nothing to lawyers, but names like Frank Garcia, Slydini, and Dai Vernon were extraordinary people who are all gone from us, yet they live on in the legends of magic.

Lou Tannen's brother owned the Circle Magic shop, where I bought my first tricks. When he realized how interested I was in magic, Mike Tannen told me that I should visit his brother's shop on 42ⁿᵈ Street. I was still a young kid, probably seven or eight. My grandfather began taking me there. Several years later, when I was probably 14 or 15, I remember speaking to Lou Tannen one time saying, "Gosh, I'd really love to work here; it would be great."

He sort of nodded and continued performing magic for his customers. Over the next few weeks, I called Mr. Tannen and said, "This is Mark Dombroff, and I'm the guy who said I'd like to work there."

I still remember the day when he said, "Well, I think I could use somebody for the summer. Come on in tomorrow, and we'll talk."

Bright and early the next day, I took the Long Island Railroad into New York City, and that started me working at Tannen's over the summers and holidays, which continued for several years, even during vacations and summers during my first year or two of college. Whenever anyone asked, I told them I worked at a publisher. Tannen's published many magic books, and I didn't want to say that I worked at a magic shop.

Those were fascinating days. I made magic in the sense that I actually built tricks in the back of the shop. I also filled orders for their huge mail-order business. Through all my activity, I hung around the legends of magic—people like Harry Loyarne, a memory expert who is now in his 90s. He was a master of card tricks, and Tannen's published several of his books. Being a part of the premier magic shop in the world was a dream for a young magician.

I was devoted to the hobby. I can say unequivocally that magic did more to prepare me to be a lawyer than any single thing in my life. It gave me the confidence to stand in front of people to speak and allowed me to be comfortable in every situation. Today, I read that the number one fear of many Americans is public speaking, which makes me even more grateful that magic has been an enormous resource for my life.

As the years have passed, my interest in magic has never waned. My collection continues to get larger because I don't think I've ever seen a magic trick that I didn't want to own. I started purchasing a lot of magic. Performance opportunities have come along frequently. I remember performing at the General Cigar Pavillion at the 1964 World's Fair in New York. I've also performed at hundreds, maybe thousands of birthday parties all over the area where I lived at various times. Growing up, the Oceanside New York Summer Recreational program gave me the opportunity to teach magic, and I bicycled, being too young to drive, to various schools for their summer recreation program. Not only was it a source of joy for me, but my confidence also grew with each performance.

Even today, I tell parents and grandparents if they have young children, to introduce magic to the kids. Encourage them to take it up as a hobby. Even after dozens of times when they ask you to watch them do a trick, grit your teeth, and enjoy it. It's more than a moment of enjoyment for them; it will build their confidence and prepare them for many experiences to come in the future. If they don't enjoy doing magic after some time, they'll drop it. Remember, nothing ventured, nothing gained.

During law school, my magic was put on a shelf. When I went to work at the FAA and then the DOJ, I picked it back up but primarily for my own amusement. During the Pago Pago case in Los Angeles (which I'll tell you about in a later chapter), I got up the nerve to audition for the Academy of Magical Arts, headquartered at the Magic Castle. The Magic Castle is a well-known private dining club for magicians in Hollywood that is still going strong. I remember the audition went well, and I became a member. I have maintained that membership to this day. I've taken clients to the Magic Castle in Hollywood over the years, and to a person, they've loved it. They have a variety of showrooms and theaters, and I have enjoyed the place, despite the fact I have to travel 3,000 miles to get there.

More of my magic collection

I also belong to other organizations for magicians, including The International Brotherhood of Magicians, the Society of American Magicians, and The Magic Circle in London, which is like the Magic Castle in some respects, except it's much older.

They have a phenomenal clubhouse and facility in London. As I write these words, last evening, I attended a video session of the Magic Collectors Corner on Zoom, which occurs every Sunday night.

My collection of magic has grown significantly over the years as my income grew. We built our house almost 15 years ago. Downstairs, I have a magic theater and library built for my collection, but it has outgrown those areas and now resides on various shelves throughout the house. As I look around my office shelves, I see many magic tricks and items. It's one of my greatest passions and one that I've enjoyed virtually my entire life.

Even more magic...

From a lawyer's perspective, most importantly, magic has allowed me to be enormously comfortable standing in front of large groups. During the last several years, I've had frequent opportunities to appear on 24/7 news channels talking about aviation. I attribute a large part of the success I've had as a "talking head" to my ability to focus on getting my message across without being nervous or concerned about the medium, whether it's a stage, a courtroom, or a television studio. This confidence can be traced to a six-year-old who developed a passion for being a magician.

Many times I've been asked to identify my favorite magic trick or effect. As I think back to what initially stimulated my interest, it was not so much the trick but rather the effect it had on me. As best I can recall, the first magic trick I ever got was the Color Vision Cube. It consisted of a small yellow plastic box with a lid that fits tightly. Inside the box was a cube with six different colors, one on each side. The spectator would take the colored cube, turn around with their back to me, and put it in the yellow box. Then they would hand it to me, and within seconds, I could identify what color was facing up, even though the lid to the box was on tightly. I still remember being mystified when the trick was first shown to me at "Magic Circle," where my grandfather had taken me.

Similarly, when I was shown something called the Square Circle, I was hooked. The trick consisted of a tube, open on both sides, that fit inside a box that had no top or bottom. Once the tube was put inside the box, after each was shown to be empty, all sorts of colored handkerchiefs could be produced.

In looking back over my magic career to identify my favorite trick, I can say that it's any trick that mystifies me; even after I understand the principle involved, I thoroughly enjoy the performance. It might be floating a woman on stage, or chopping off someone's head with a guillotine, or making people appear or disappear; the answer is not so much the trick as the performance. It's the performance that I enjoy the most about magic.

Certainly, one has to "practice, practice, practice" to have complete confidence in presenting the magic effect to spectators. What keeps me hooked is the response I get when the trick is properly performed and presented. That is when I get the most enjoyment. The process is similar to "preparing, preparing, preparing" for a case or trial, and getting the result from a judge or jury that you wanted. The similarity between performing magic and being in a courtroom is what has drawn me to both disciplines.

FAA and DOJ: For the United States...

I spent most of my time in college, enjoying the experience, and didn't give much consideration to a career until my senior year was coming to a close. Ultimately, the choice was law school, and I remained in Washington and attended the Washington College Law School, which is part of American University. Since I stayed on the same campus, my fraternity brothers were still around, but the study and requirements of law school were consuming.

At one point during law school, I had to take a leave of absence. It was the late 60s, and our country was heavily involved in the Vietnam War, and I joined the reserves. During my second year of law school, orders came to report for basic training at Fort Ord in California. After five months, I returned to law school in Washington and fulfilled my reserve duty, first with a National Guard unit out of West Chester, Pennsylvania, and then the DC National Guard, doing one weekend a month for drills. That particular unit in DC was a military police unit and has been in the news recently because of the demonstrators in D.C.

Life takes interesting turns sometimes. One of the major attractions to the law for me was an early fascination with *Perry Mason* and his exploits in criminal cases. Upon graduating from law school in 1970, it would seem to make sense I would gravitate to criminal law. Yet, I've spent my entire legal career in the aviation area. That was never my intention, but it sort of just happened.

The process of looking for a job began during my third year of law school. Schoolwork, during my final year of law school, was relatively easy, so I was looking for a part-time job. In one of the campus buildings, they had a bulletin board where people posted job openings, usually on three by five index cards. In those days, there was no placement office, on-campus interviews, or any other type of recruiting. We were on our own when it came to finding a job.

I located a posting for a part-time law clerk for a lawyer in Bethesda, Maryland. It turned out that it was from the Washington Counsel for the Aircraft Owners and Pilots Association (AOPA). AOPA is made up of private pilots and is a powerful lobbying organization for the interests of general aviation pilots around the country. I was nearing graduation from law school and had only been on an airplane once in my life to go to Florida for a fraternity convention during college. Riding the train was how I went back and forth to home in New York.

While working for this lawyer, I was exposed to a variety of things in the aviation area, and I enjoyed the work. Approaching the completion of law school, I didn't have a job, and the lawyer I was working for wasn't in a position to hire anyone full-time, so I started looking elsewhere. My search began with a trip to the library—remember, this was in the late

60s, long before computers. I secured a volume from a set of huge books called "Martindale-Hubbell Law Directory" that provides background information on lawyers and law firms in the United States. They are listed geographically, so I identified all the possibilities around the Washington area.

I sat in my apartment and copied the names of law firms and government agencies that I might be interested in pursuing and read a little about their practice. When I finished, I had a list of 300 law firms and government agencies. I wrote a cover letter, worked up a resume, and took them to a typing service where they were addressed and printed. Remember, this was in the days before computers. A couple of weeks later, I picked them up, signed each of them by hand, placed a stamp on the envelope, and dropped them in the mail.

In a couple of weeks, I was inundated with mail. Every single letter was a rejection. I obviously had no idea how the recruiting process worked for lawyers. One letter indicated they had no openings but appreciated my interest. It also noted that if I found myself in the vicinity of their office, feel free to stop by, and they would be happy to visit. It came from the Federal Aviation Administration. I genuinely thought they meant it. Much later, it occurred to me that it was nothing more than a form letter, no different than the others, just a little more polite.

Thankfully, at the time, I didn't know any better, and I called them. The woman who signed the letter, as I recall, was the Administrative Head of the General Counsel's office at the FAA. I called and told her that I received her letter and would love to stop by and meet them. I'm confident there were some raised eyebrows about this law student who didn't recognize he was being brushed off. So, I traveled to 800 Independence

Avenue and introduced myself. We talked for a few minutes before she advised me it was my lucky day. Someone had just turned down a job, and they wanted to speak to me about the position. That's how I got into aviation!

It could easily have been another agency or other law firm. Perhaps the reason I even knew the FAA existed was because of my clerkship for AOPA. I'm sure it helped some, but really, I was in the right place at the right time.

Thus, I began my career in 1970 as an attorney with the FAA. I was first hired as a GS-11 government employee, but between the time I was hired and the time I started working, I had yet to pass the bar, so I was technically a law clerk. I actually began at the FAA before I was a member of the bar. I was assigned to the "General Law" section. However, because of my *Perry Mason* upbringing, I knew I was in the wrong place. I wanted to practice trial law. I wanted to be *Perry Mason*.

As quickly as possible, I undertook efforts to get moved to the Litigation Division of the General Counsel's Office. That's where I wanted to be. It didn't take long to be transferred there, but then I encountered another problem. The Litigation Division of the FAA doesn't litigate! The FAA is the client, and those who litigate on behalf of all government agencies are at the Department of Justice. Our role at FAA was that of in-house counsel. For example, if the government was sued because of allegations of air traffic control negligence, we would support the Department of Justice litigators.

Under the law, the Attorney General and the Department of Justice is the attorney for the United States. The various United States Attorney's offices around the country are the local representatives of the DOJ. I quickly realized that I was not in a position to litigate cases, and I needed to be at the DOJ.

I had a friend from law school who had been a helicopter pilot in Vietnam. He was a very bright guy and ended up working at the DOJ Aviation Unit, a small office at Justice that handled all the aviation cases. I was working as an in-house counsel for the FAA, and he was where I wanted to be. Shortly after a year at the FAA, my friend helped make it possible for me to transfer to the Department of Justice.

Although I was based in Washington, I constantly traveled around the country, defending the United States. It's essential to understand how this works with our legal system. Historically, the U.S. has a Common Law system that came from England. That system prohibited lawsuits against the King, or in our situation, lawsuits against the government.

For example, if you walked into the Post Office, slipped, and broke your leg, you were not allowed to sue the government even if they were negligent by not keeping the floor dry. The only way to get relief required a unique and complex system. It entailed contacting your Congressman and convincing him/her to introduce a private relief bill in Congress. Typically, the bill would be added as an amendment to other legislation, and if it passed, you would be awarded money.

In 1945, a B-25 Bomber encountered fog and crashed into the side of the Empire State Building. The pilot asked for clearance to land but was told there was no visibility. However, he continued, and the fog disoriented him, took a wrong turn, and smashed into the building between the 78th and 80th floors. One engine flew through the entire building and out the other side before falling 900 feet to the roof of a nearby building. After everything was sorted out, fourteen people were killed, numerous suffered severe injuries, and there was extensive property damage.

Some of those suffering losses refused to accept settlements offered by the government. The result was the passage of legislation the following year, the Federal Tort Claims Act, that allowed citizens to sue the government for negligence. The FAA was deeply involved because they operate the air traffic control system for the country. The Act was made retroactive to cover the accident in 1945. From that point forward, private citizens and corporations have been allowed to sue the U.S. in cases of negligence.

There are exceptions and limitations, but because it is now possible to sue the Federal Government, there is a need for government lawyers to litigate these cases. Any suits involving the FAA are handled by the Aviation Unit of the DOJ. These included allegations of being negligent in providing weather support services for the military, incidents when it was asserted government aviation activity failed and caused a loss, and virtually any type of air disaster that caused damage or death. I spent 15 years working in the Aviation Unit, the last five of which I was first the Assistant Director for Aviation, and then I was named the Director of Aviation. Eventually, Admiralty, which dealt with maritime matters, was combined with aviation, and my office became known as the "crash and splash" unit and continues to exist today.

During one of my many trips while at DOJ, I traveled to San Francisco for a court appearance. Before returning home, there was a bomb scare focused on a TWA aircraft. Something about a bomb being found in the cockpit. Since I opted not to fly TWA home, I changed plans and flights, which meant a stopover in Chicago. On my new flight on American Airlines, I met a flight attendant, and we ended up having coffee together while at O'Hare. This was in the fall of 1972. She was living and flying out of Boston, and before we departed, I got her phone number and address.

My wife Jan

Later that year, I was trying a case in Santa Fe, New Mexico, and we arranged for her to come to Washington for a visit when I returned home. She was at the airport, standing outside the gate when I arrived. By this time, it was late in 1972. On January 4, 1973, we were married, and as I write this, Jan and I have been together for more than 47 years, and have a wonderful daughter, Jessica.

I stayed at the DOJ until 1985. Since beginning with the FAA in 1970,

My daughter Jessica

I assumed I would stay with the government for a couple of years and then gravitate into private practice. However, I so thoroughly enjoyed being with the DOJ and defending the U.S., my two or three years turned into fifteen.

By that time, I had gone as high as possible without entering the political ranks. As Director of Aviation and Admiralty, I was part of a small group of five Directors who reported to a Deputy Assistant Attorney General. Virtually everything above that was a political appointment. There was simply no place to go after 15 years. I recall I was earning $61,000 as a member of the Senior Executive Service, a Director with offices in New York, San Francisco, and Washington reporting to me, and I was topped out salary-wise. I was married, and my daughter, Jessica, was four years old.

It was definitely time to consider private practice.

Into the Private Sector

It was 1985, and my two or three years of working for the government had turned into fifteen. In my experience, the people running the Department of Justice were true professionals, even the political appointees. Once confirmed, they typically left the politics behind and were very capable at their jobs.

By that time, I had written several books for lawyers. All of them focused on practice techniques and strategies and were published specifically for the legal profession. Also, I was enjoying frequent speaking around the country. During one of those speeches, I met an attorney who was doing product liability defense work with a law firm Hughes Hubbard & Reed, a prominent firm in New York. During our conversation, I indicated some interest in private practice, and the result was an invitation to interview in their Washington office.

Their Washington office was solid, led by Phil Lacovara, who had been with the Department of Justice. He worked with the Solicitor General's office, handling appeals from the DOJ. Phil had, as part of the Watergate team, argued the case involving an 18-minute gap in the Nixon tapes case before the U.S. Supreme Court. That was the case where Rosemary Woods,

President Nixon's secretary, alleged that she had inadvertently erased several minutes of the infamous Watergate tapes.

A couple of other DOJ alumni were in the Washington office, which made it comfortable to join them. None of us had been in private practice before joining Hughes Hubbard & Reed. It was the first time I was required to get clients and ask for business. While I had developed many relationships among high profile people in the aviation industry, now I had the task of turning those relationships into a successful private practice.

Many of those relationships were with insurance markets. Frequently, whenever airlines were sued for negligence, the lawsuit included the United States Government, so it was common that we were co-defendants with airlines, manufacturers, and other aviation companies. Since I knew them, I began making phone calls and traveling to meet with the people I knew.

Numerous trips were made to London, where, fortunately, the entire insurance market is concentrated in the same area. It's called the *City*, and it's where the Lloyds of London and the insurance market are located. To understand how this works, realize that Lloyds is not a single insurance company. It's a marketplace where individual syndicates write insurance under the Lloyds umbrella, created by the Lloyds Act in 1871 by the British Parliament. Each syndicate typically consists of multiple financial backers who are grouped into individual syndicates. When they write a policy, it provides a means of spreading the risk. Although it began primarily to serve maritime needs, it has dramatically expanded over the years and is a natural fit for the airline industry.

We tend to think of insurance companies operating like Allstate or State Farm auto insurance, where one company provides coverage for our vehicle for a few thousand dollars. It's quick and easy, only 15 minutes on the phone is what they advertise. However, airline insurance does not deal with thousand dollar amounts or even millions of dollars. In today's world, airlines are insured for billions of dollars, far more potential liability than one insurance company wants to insure. The way these huge policies get written is that a broker, a Lloyds of London qualified insurance broker, acting on behalf of the airline or aircraft manufacturer, will literally walk around to various syndicates in the Lloyds building. The syndicates occupy or sit in places called *boxes*, two or more wooden benches facing one another with big tables between them. The underwriters and claims people for the syndicates are sitting in their boxes.

The broker approaches the boxes seeking underwriters to take a share of the risk. It might be five or ten percent or more, maybe even less. They indicate, on a piece of paper called a *slip*, what percentage of the risk they will take, and hand it to the broker. The broker then continues to other syndicates, and in the area around Lloyds in the *City*, to insurance companies, to secure 100% coverage. They walk around until they have one hundred percent. Once accomplished, a lead insurer is designated, and they are responsible for managing the risk on behalf of all the participating syndicates.

It's a complex process that has worked well for centuries. I had become very familiar with the whole process, and all the people, including brokers, involved with Lloyds. I was also familiar with companies both in the U.S. and elsewhere. With the advent of technology, the insurance industry has become more complicated, but Lloyds is bound up in tradition. That's how I started building my practice… by working with contacts

I already knew. Although I was working with a large law firm, my only responsibility was to build the aviation area.

Hughes Hubbard & Reed was very supportive. I wasn't experienced or knowledgeable regarding law firm economics or management issues. I wanted my focus to be on building a law practice dealing with aviation. There was another firm in New York working in aviation that had been around for a long time. They put together and sponsored an annual conference, and because of my work at DOJ, I was frequently invited to participate. I had agreed to speak at a session one year that was going to be held in Marbella, Spain. After I accepted their invitation, I made the decision to go into private practice.

I flew to London and from there, connected with a flight to Spain for the conference. The immigration authorities in Spain would not allow me to enter the country, which didn't make sense. The explanation was that I still had an official U.S. Government passport, but was no longer a government employee. I had failed to obtain a regular blue passport and didn't have a visa necessary for going to Spain on an official passport. Essentially, they deported me and put me back on the same British Airways plane. When I arrived back in London, it was near midnight. I located a hotel near the airport and began to devise a plan. Do I need to return to Washington, or is there something else I can do?

It was Sunday, and the next day was a bank holiday in England, and everything would be closed. I called the Spanish Embassy to see if anything can be done to help. Someone answered the phone, and I explained the whole story. I don't know if I was speaking with a member of the maintenance staff or someone from security or whatever, but I said I urgently needed to talk to the legal attaché. I left my phone number and expressed appreciation if I could get a call.

Within an hour, the legal attaché from the Spanish Embassy was on the phone. Even though they were closed the next day, he asked me to come to the back door at 1 p.m. and ring the bell. I did, and much to my shock, they handed me a visa. I was able to get on the same flight as the day before and flew back to Spain. Sure enough, I encountered the same immigration officer, this time with a quizzical look on his face, but he stamped my passport, and I was on my way.

When I spoke at the conference, I announced my new position at Hughes Hubbard & Reed. Thanking them for their support, I reminded them that I looked forward to continuing to work together in the future. Back in London waiting for my flight home in a day, I wandered around the insurance market. At a pub, I ran into the senior partner with the New York law firm that sponsored the program and had invited me. He told me I would never succeed practicing aviation law in Washington D.C. I will always remember those words.

The practice grew, and I hired several lawyers, including two for the New York office of Hughes Hubbard & Reed, and two more for the Miami office. My first client was Piper Aircraft. They wanted assistance with issues they had with the National Transportation Safety Board that investigates all aviation accidents. It helped that I knew everyone at the NTSB and DOJ. Even today, I continue to maintain those relationships.

A London aviation company called and asked for help. They had a case in upstate New York that had been pending for years and wanted me to take charge of representation. When they sent the information about the situation, I realized I could resolve the matter very quickly. When it comes to insurance clients, they want cases closed as rapidly as possible. I made a few phone calls and reported in a couple of days that the matter was settled. The case was dismissed.

In the summer of 1988, about three years after I joined Hughes Hubbard, Phil Lacovara came into my office and closed the door. He told me of his plan to go to General Electric to become their head of litigation. For me, all I cared about was building my practice, so I congratulated him. Another one of the partners became the managing partner of my office in D.C., a former Justice Department guy, and I happily continued doing what I was doing… building a practice.

A short time later, I was flying to San Francisco. Back in those days, phones on airplanes were located in the back of the seat in front of you, and I called my wife from the airplane. She reported that the head of the litigation department at Hughes Hubbard & Reed had called. He was in New York and was a person I would never deal with normally, so I called him from the plane. He told me what I already knew, that Phil Locavara was leaving the firm. He also revealed that a much larger group of lawyers was also leaving the Washington office. I thanked him for the call and continued with my business in San Francisco.

When I returned to the office, I became, by default, the managing partner of the D.C. office of Hughes Hubbard & Reed. The firm was a very traditional Wall Street law firm, and I don't think management was ever very happy about me, basically, an insurance defense lawyer as the managing partner. I wasn't sure what the future was for me because they wanted some changes that made it difficult for me. The firm's billing rates were high, and they wanted me to charge those high rates to the insurance companies, but it would price me out of the market. Moreover, my focus was on building a practice and not managing an office.

After a matter of weeks, I called a headhunter in Washington and outlined our practice and asked if she could help relocate my team and practice. She reached out to several law firms, and I ended up interviewing with a firm based in Chicago called Katten Muchin & Zavis. They had no presence outside Chicago, but they wanted to expand. During the interview, they made me feel very much at home, and I genuinely liked them. I had a couple of lawyers in New York and Miami, and a bunch in Washington. Katten Muchin & Zavis greatly wanted to become a national firm, especially in Los Angeles and Washington, but they didn't feel New York was the place to be since the competition was too great. That's probably true, even today. Unless you can compete at the top of the legal profession, New York is a tough market.

After several meetings and discussions, I took my entire practice, all the lawyers from New York, Miami, and Washington and joined Katten. I remember the day I received the offer letter that explained the details. It indicated I would be on the firm's executive committee, and the office in Washington would be known as Katten Muchin Zavis & Dombroff. It had never even occurred to me to even ask for these two things. We opened our offices in Washington, New York, and Miami all on the same day, and I was the managing partner.

The space we leased in Washington was in the building next to Hughes Hubbard & Reed, so I ended up moving next door. It was a wonderful environment. We ended up joining another firm that had about 250 lawyers, and I continued with a higher profile in the legal profession. Other than one partner, I was a top biller in the firm and had one of the biggest books of business. Later, we merged with a California firm in Los Angeles. The attorney running that office practiced criminal defense and had defended John DeLorean in a famous drug case and won an acquittal, but I was always concerned about that merger since, in almost every way, the firm continued to be Chicago "centric."

There was no doubt that Katten was a Chicago firm. The leadership consisted of Illinois lawyers, and it was the center of their universe. Michael Zavis and Alan Muchin were the powers in the firm. They represented the Chicago Bulls and the White Sox, and Alan Muchin was a partner in the Bulls. Everything about the firm breathed Chicago, yet the second biggest biller was me, and aviation was the fastest-growing part of the practice.

Eventually, Katten wanted to compete with the big, storied Chicago firms. Even though they were successful, they were still the upstarts on the block. They wanted the same client base and to recruit out of the same law schools. Consequently, to pay first-year lawyers and all lawyers equivalently, hourly rates have to increase. I didn't need to raise my billing rates because I couldn't raise my billing rates to the level Katten was raising them. I told them it was unacceptable, and I wasn't going to do it, and it became a point of contention.

In May of 1994, Michael Zavis called and told me that I had to meet with the executive committee, so I flew to Chicago. We met in a hotel suite, and the discussion was essential that my practice and the firm had grown apart. We spoke about the economics, but what I *heard* was that I was next in line to be managing partner when Zavis retired, and that was unacceptable. The center of their universe would no longer have been Chicago. No matter how high profile they became, I would have been an insurance defense lawyer managing the firm. After a day of discussion, we agreed to separate.

We reached an extraordinarily generous agreement. The Firm agreed to waive any notice period and release my entire team, which by then was twelve or thirteen lawyers, including my people in Chicago. They refunded my equity buy-in with a lump sum payment as opposed to paying it out over time under the partnership agreement. We were allowed to stay in our offices for six months, rent-free. With client approval, all our cases were transferred to us, and Katten Muchin provided an interest-free loan for one year in the high six figures. They even hired and paid for a consultant to help make the transition to a new firm.

Everything stayed in place—all our lawyers, even filing cabinets, had six months to transition. Katten Muchin & Zavis were remarkably generous and did everything in an extraordinarily classy way. In the end, I believe the idea of somebody in Washington leading a Chicago-centric firm was totally unacceptable. Ironically, years later, that's exactly what happened... a partner in the Washington office became managing partner. I guess I was ahead of my time.

On July 16, 1994, I started Dombroff & Gilmore. I had hired Patricia Gilmore at the Department of Justice from a law firm in San Francisco when I was at Hughes Hubbard. She moved with me to Katten, and together we founded Dombroff & Gilmore.

One of the most interesting cases we handled was for a company named Blackwater. It was founded by Erik Prince, who was a Navy Seal when the USS Cole was attacked in October of 2000. The ship, a missile destroyer operated by the Navy, was being refueled in Yemen. The attack was carried out by a small group on a suicide mission. They approached the ship in a small fiberglass boat filled with C4 explosives. The result was a gaping hole in the side of the USS Cole and the death of 17 sailors and injuries to 39 others. Prince was concerned that the sailors on board were not adequately trained in dealing with potential terrorist attacks. He left the Seals and founded Blackwater.

The purpose of Blackwater was to provide anti-terrorism training, and he secured a number of government contracts to provide training. Many went through the Blackwater training, both military and non-military. Blackwater created a facility located on the border between North Carolina and Virginia. I had the opportunity to visit the facility, not as a student, but rather as an attorney for the company. It was an impressive place with firing ranges and driving courses and all sorts of sophisticated resources used to train military and non-military classified personnel from all over the world.

When the war on terror became full-blown after 9/11, Blackwater was given many contracts to provide security and protection in Iraq and Afghanistan. There were many issues, and the contracts were large. Our involvement occurred because Blackwater had purchased Presidential Airways. Previously, Presidential operated as a passenger airline out of Dulles Airport. As I recall, Presidential went defunct and filed bankruptcy. The asset that made Presidential Airlines attractive to Blackwater was their operating certificate issued by the FAA.

Blackwater moved the operation to Melbourne, Florida, and continued to service government contracts, which included providing aviation logistical support in Afghanistan and elsewhere. Flying aircraft in a war zone will often lead to a crash, and that's precisely what happened to a Presidential Casa 212 aircraft. It was carrying three soldiers back to their assigned base when it crashed into the side of a mountain, part of a box canyon. The soldiers and all three crew members were killed. Relatives filed a lawsuit against Presidential Airlines in October 2005, in Tampa, Florida.

According to the investigative report from the NTSB, the Blackwater pilots were unprofessional in flying low through the canyon. The crash led to extensive debate over the use of private military contractors in war zones. McKenna Long & Aldridge, a law firm in Washington, represented Blackwater in some aspects of the case, and I was invited to interview at the Blackwater corporate headquarters about the possibility of handling the aviation aspects of the case. I clearly remember the experience because it was during one of our *Aviation Symposiums*, and during a break in the program, I walked across the street to their office for the interview. They hired us.

I was familiar with McKenna Long & Aldridge, having encountered them when I was at the Department of Justice. They built their reputation on government contract law. Since maritime was also under my charge at Justice, I was involved with contracts concerning submarines manufactured by their client General Dynamics.

To make a long story short, we successfully settled the case against Presidential. Blackwater was very happy, and we continued to do work for Presidential. To this day, I represent them, although they've gone through several owners since Erik Prince. Today, they are owned by a company out of Chicago.

In 2014, I received a phone call from the folks at McKenna Long. As I indicated previously, I knew of them but had not had much dealing with them. My firm of Dombroff Gilmore had offices in New York, Miami, Chicago, and Washington and had grown to more than 15 lawyers.

U.S. Airways went through a period where they had several catastrophic accidents. I had taken cases to trial that we couldn't get settled, significantly large cases where plaintiffs were seeking punitive damages against the airline. I believe it's true to this day; I'm the only lawyer who has taken a major airline through a jury verdict on punitive damages case with a successful verdict.

McKenna Long said they had a large aerospace client base in government contracts. They knew that I did a lot of work for big aerospace manufacturers. Other than matters relative to government contracts, they didn't do anything else for their aviation clients. They were interested in our full-service aviation practice.

Remember, this is 2014, and by that time, the only major catastrophic accident for the past several years was Colgan Air in Buffalo, New York. Aviation had become a remarkably safe industry, particularly in the United States. When I started my firm, we had three major catastrophic accidents I was defending at the same time. They involved hundreds of deaths and huge pieces of litigation. That had all changed over the years, and I already had the philosophy expressed through our creating the *Aviation Symposium*, of not waiting for someone to have an accident before they hire you. I didn't want to wait until the accident. I wanted to be in the board room so they would know me before the accident.

I had a case where an airline asked us to come to the city where an accident investigation was underway, two weeks after the accident. Everyone was still on the scene, and they wanted to interview us to possibly represent them. That's the worst possible time to first meet your attorney. It's not a context that builds confidence, and there is no opportunity to train people as to what is going to unfold after an accident.

We are an aviation industry practice that understands the entire industry. McKenna Long, who already handled government contracts, approached us because they wanted to be a full-service aviation practice. They wanted us to merge because it gave them instant credibility. That made positive sense to me. At the same time, I was thinking about what I wanted to do now. My firm was 19 years old; I had been in the industry since 1970, and now it has evolved into a very safe industry. It was time to reflect on my next move.

Do I want to add more practices? We were already spread out, and I was reluctant to open up in California. It's challenging to manage an office 3,000 miles away. Do I want to merge with somebody? Do I want to be merged? Out of the blue, the McKenna Long guys called me. I had lunch with two of them, and I ended up interviewing with a bunch of them, and it made sense. We merged, and the Dombroff & Gilmore offices became McKenna Long offices.

We were already profitable, but the whole concept was they would open up their aerospace client base to us and make introductions that would give us, and them, much more business. However, it didn't happen. A frequent problem with law firms is the lack of internal marketing. They hire lawyers who bring a book of clients with them, but they don't know how to market to expand the business with the new clients internally. Although the client might be happy with your work, there are other areas where the firm could help them, but no one tries to market these new services.

For internal marketing to be successful, partners who work with a particular client must be willing to share the client with other partners who can help them. They have to make introductions. What we discovered with our new partners is that they were either reluctant or slow to open up these relationships, and it was very frustrating.

The Dombroff Gilmore *Aviation Symposium* continued and became the McKenna Long *Aviation Symposium*. We never missed a beat and were just as successful. We branded the McKenna Long Aviation practice, but I continued to be frustrated because they wouldn't open up their clients to us.

After about a year and a half, they were becoming more responsive, but then we began to hear rumors there're they were having merger discussions with another law firm. One of the things that was so attractive to me at McKenna Long was that they wanted a full-service aviation firm like ours. To me, that was the number one priority in agreeing to the McKenna Long deal. Several months after the rumors started, a merger vote was put to the partners, and they voted not to merge. The firm they were talking with was of no interest to me, and they had no particular interest in an aviation practice.

After the merger was rejected, McKenna Long management, unbeknownst to a lot of the partners and me, continued to have discussions with the other firm. The ones who didn't want to merge eventually left McKenna. The problem for me was that among those who left were the ones who initially wanted me to be part of the firm. The merger was brought up again and disappointingly approved because those who opposed it were gone. I found myself at a law firm that didn't have an aerospace client base and no particular interest in growing that practice. McKenna Long merged, and we had to decide what to do.

The new firm was not the type of firm that fits with us, so we started to ask around and discuss law firms that would be better for our practice. A good thing about an aviation practice is that it can be a stand-alone practice.

Our search for a new firm led us to LeClair Ryan, and we joined them in 2017. They were very supportive of our practice, and we continued with the *Aviation Symposium* and grew even more. They were supportive as it continued to grow, and saw the power of bringing hundreds of potential clients together with us being the only lawyers in the room.

What we didn't know when we joined, and in some respects, this was my fault, was that the foundation of LeClair Ryan had problems. Financial issues presented themselves, lawyers were leaving the firm, and in 2017, LeClair Ryan reached an agreement with a non-lawyer legal services firm that provided various services to law firms that were promised to deliver great benefits to both. It never happened.

In early 2019, we left LeClair Ryan, and we once again found ourselves in a place we never anticipated. The search for a new firm resumed. I made a phone call to Fox Rothschild on a Sunday, and I reached out to the Chairman of the firm. I had spoken to them about a year and a half earlier, and I asked if they were still interested. He assured me that he was still interested in our practice.

At the end of August 2019, we joined Fox Rothschild—our entire team—including our administrative and support staff for our lawyers, including everyone in Florida and New York. Since the time we were first Dombroff Gilmore, then merged

The three of us

with McKenna Long, which evolved into another firm, then moved to LeClair Ryan, and now we're Fox Rothschild.

The main reason I want to be a part of another firm at this stage of my career is that I didn't like waking up in the middle of the night worrying about having enough money to pay all the overhead of the business of law. Rent, secretary salaries, workers' comp, insurance, and all the other necessities of the running of a business—I wanted to be free of all of that. I wanted to have a support structure around me and a client base or potential pool of clients that I could focus on developing. I quickly tired of all the administrative stuff. I want my attention to go to two things: developing business and practicing law.

Everyone who knows me, knows Bo!

US Airways Flight 405: The Perfect Question and the "Wow" Factor

Every trial lawyer dreams about the opportunity to ask the perfect question that will change the entire tenor of the trial. It might be a witness making an unexpected confession to a crime, a witness caught in a lie, or explosive information that sends the trial off in a new direction. Although they seem to happen all the time on TV and in the movies, they are not that common in the real world. When they do, it is certainly memorable.

One of the big airline accidents I handled in private practice involved US Airways 405. The plane was a Fokker F28, about the size of one of the regional jets that are flown today. It is uncommon to see an F28 flying in the US now, but this was 1992.

The case involved Flight 405 that originated in Jacksonville, Florida, and landed in the snow at LaGuardia, slightly over an hour late. Fifty-eight of the sixty-two passengers on board deplaned in New York, grabbed their luggage, and headed out into the snow. Forty-two were waiting at LaGuardia to take their place at Gate B1 for the final leg of the flight scheduled to land in Cleveland.

However, the terminus for Flight 405 on March 22, 1992, was not Cleveland. Instead, it was Flushing Bay near the end of the LaGuardia runway. The plane rolled down the runway and began to rise above the ground, but it could not get enough lift to stay in the air. Although it was in late March, wintry weather was a problem, not that uncommon for the Northeast.

Flight delays are a regular occurrence for airline pilots, and Captain Wally Majure had a reputation of wanting to please his passengers. He spoke often and proudly about the airline's on-time record. It was also no secret that he did not enjoy the packed skies above LaGuardia, reportedly telling his fiancé once that LaGuardia was "an accident waiting to happen." (N.R Kleinfield, New York Times, *The Ordinary Turned to Instant Horror for All Aboard US Airways's Flight 405*, March 29, 1992)

Ice on the wings is a serious concern for any plane flying in cold, wet weather. Any ice or frost disrupts airflow over the surface of the wing and reduces lift. De-icer is used to keep the wings free of ice. Depending on the conditions, one treatment might only remain effective for a few minutes. On Flight 405, de-icing was completed at 8:26 pm. A delay caused the Captain to request a second de-icing.

Multiple de-icings were made on the plane before it left the runway, but there was a significant amount of time that passed before the plane taxied down the runway for takeoff at about 9:00 pm. Snow was falling, and the temperature was just below freezing at 31 degrees. The crash investigation revealed it was ice that kept the plane from getting off the ground.

Unable to stay in the air, the plane veered off to the left, struck several objects before finally stopping in Flushing Bay near the end of the runway. Fifty-one passengers were on board, and 27 were killed in the crash, including the Captain.

All the typical procedures and precautions were followed in getting the plane ready to fly before it ever pulled away from the gate. The investigation focused on the efficacy of the de-icing fluid, which ultimately brought about significant changes in the way planes were prepared during wintry conditions. It was a watershed accident in terms of understanding de-icing.

As you can imagine, there was a great deal of litigation filed against the airline. It was all brought together and consolidated in Federal Court in Cleveland. That particular court made sense because that's where the plane was headed. The largest number of passenger deaths were people headed home from New York, where they had been for business reasons.

Judge Thomas Lambros was assigned the consolidated case. He was an interesting judge, and I spent many weeks in his court over the next couple of years. He had a reputation of shortening and simplifying the legal process, which was evident as he constantly encouraged us to reach a settlement in this case. The airline and its insurers tried hard to make that happen, but the plaintiffs were not interested.

Generally, airlines will settle cases and claims with passengers. The ticket you purchase is a contract that says, in so many words, the airline will get you from Point A to Point B, and they will do it safely. When they fail, it is a breach of contract, and it's an essentially absolute contractual liability. There is no limit on the amount of compensatory damages that can be recovered because it's a function of how much you can prove.

It takes into account your medical expenses, lost income, future lost earnings, and other considerations. The numbers can be substantial, and we tried hard to come to settlements.

But, we couldn't settle the case because the plaintiff's lawyers wanted punitive damages. These were damages, not meant to compensate for a loss, but rather to punish the airline. The airline was willing to pay for damages but had no intention of paying punitive damages. When deciding on damages, there are two standards. The first is simple negligence, which refers to making a mistake. People make mistakes all the time, and there is nothing malicious about them. The second standard is recklessness to such a degree that it should be punished.

The plaintiffs were claiming there was conduct that should be punished, and they wanted numbers so high that we couldn't settle. There was nothing to punish here. Mistakes were made, but they were not intentional or reckless. We admitted from the beginning that people make mistakes; they are not intentionally doing it, not acting recklessly, just made a mistake. We said they should award compensatory damages, but not punitive damages. Since we were unable to settle, the case was set for a jury trial in Cleveland.

It was obvious to me during our preparations that I needed to identify experts who would testify on behalf of the airline. It's common, in both civil and criminal cases, to have fact witnesses and expert witnesses. A fact witness is someone with firsthand knowledge regarding the events, and expert witnesses, who aren't involved in the underlying events, take the facts and circumstances testified to by others and testify to opinions based on their training and experience.

My job, defending the airline, was to identify the appropriate experts in the essential areas that help the jury better understand the case. As I began thinking about an expert in this case that was headed to a jury verdict, it was clear I wanted an expert who had knowledge and expertise, along with unassailable credentials. However, I wanted more. I wanted someone who had a "wow" factor that might set the tone for the entire jury.

What was so significant is that we were going to try punitive damages against an airline. This was rather unprecedented, so I was focused on presenting an unprecedented defense.

As I thought about flying and the aerospace industry generally, it dawned on me that it would be great to get someone from NASA, perhaps even an astronaut. A colleague, who was a defense lawyer, had represented McDonnell Douglas, an aircraft manufacturer. One of their senior vice-presidents at the time was Charles "Pete" Conrad. He was an astronaut in the Apollo program on the Apollo 12 mission and walked on the moon with his shipmate, Alan Bean.

If you read Tom Clancy's book, *The Right Stuff*, I think Pete is literally talked about on the first page. Conrad began his military career as a test pilot and flight instructor for the Navy in 1953. In 1962, he was selected to be a member of the second group of astronauts and took part in several experiments during the Gemini 5 flight, one of which was a record at the time of spaceflight of more than 190 hours.

In 1969, Conrad and Alan Bean journeyed to the moon and spent thirty-one and a half hours on the moon surface. In 1974, he retired from the Navy and eventually took an executive position with McDonnell Douglas. When I was introduced to

Conrad by my friend, he was thinking about retirement in the not-too-distant future. For all the things you could say about Conrad, the plain and simple truth is that he was a pilot.

I couldn't think of anyone better or any type of person better suited to be an expert than an astronaut who possessed all the highest technical qualifications. He also had an airline transport pilot certificate, the same certificate that all airline pilots possess.

Conrad and I spoke several times, and I described the role of an expert witness. As we progressed, he became more and more enthused about being an expert. I remember, probably about a year before the trial, as we got more and more serious about his testimony, he decided he needed to fly the F28 aircraft, which he had never flown before. I made arrangements for him to go out with the US Airways' pilots and fly the plane.

I always keep a trial notebook with a section for each witness, both direct and cross-examinations. There is a section for jury selection, opening arguments, closing arguments, and every other part of a trial. I start building that notebook almost as soon as we get hired, just in case it goes to trial. It is used to collect and organize information as it unfolds through discovery depositions and document production. In the section I made for Pete Conrad in the event he ever got to testify at a trial in front of a jury, I had a series of questions, including the first question.

"Sir, have you ever walked on the moon?"

I wrote it in my notes, not that I could forget it, because I felt that asking that question in front of the jury was going to grab their attention as nothing could ever grab their attention.

On a side note, Pete Conrad and his wife Nancy became good friends of mine. Pete died tragically following a motorcycle accident, which, in some respects, is the way he would have wanted to go. Nancy continues to be a friend, and I'm on the Advisory Board of The Conrad Foundation.

The case progressed with depositions and sworn testimony outside the courtroom that could be used to discover what witnesses think or know, to determine how they will testify at trial. The plaintiff's lawyers took Pete's deposition, and he expressed his opinions regarding the performance of the flight crew and airline.

The tone of the trial was set during the opening statements. It was a single trial on liability, and, if in fact, the plaintiffs prevailed, then each case would have a separate damages trial. The jury knew they were trying liability, including punitive conduct.

I told the jury during my opening statement that they should award the plaintiff compensatory damages. I told them they should find that the airline made a mistake and breached its Contract of Passage. I told them they should also find the airline was negligent, but there was no punitive conduct, no basis for a finding of punitive conduct or punitive damages, and no reason to punish the airline.

This plan admitting negligence was a subject of lengthy discussions with the airline and the insurance company before the trial ever began. I remember making this point in the courtroom with many of the deceased passengers' families and the injured passengers in attendance. Perhaps not surprisingly, their attorney objected to the fact that I was admitting liability for compensatory damages for negligence. We knew that if we communicated this fact very clearly to the jury, it would remove the sting from the conduct of the airline and make it much more difficult for the jury to award punitive damages based on punishing the airline.

The plaintiff's objection was vociferous, so we went to a sidebar at the bench, out of the jury's hearing. The judge asked about their objection.

The attorney answered, "Well, he's admitting negligence to make it more difficult to get punitive damages."

The judge looked at him in some amazement and informed him there was no basis for the objection. I also recall that he looked at me and said something like "Nicely done," before adding, "You may continue, Mr. Dombroff."

When it was time to call my experts, after two weeks of the plaintiff's case, I called "Mr. Charles Conrad Jr." Pete was a relatively short man, with incredibly wild eyebrows and a gap in his front top teeth, certainly not the Tom Cruz type you would expect to see as a Top Gun fighter pilot.

He took the stand, but the jury, after weeks of testimony, didn't recognize the name Charles Conrad Jr. At that point, I asked the question I had been waiting several years to ask, "Sir, have you ever walked on the moon?"

When he said, "Yes," you could almost hear the breath leave the courtroom as all of a sudden, people recognized and understood who and what was sitting in front of them—a genuine American hero.

Then I said, "We'll come back to that, sir," and continued asking a series of qualifying questions about his training, education, and work experience. When we were in recess, and the jury was out of the room, I remember the judge wanted his picture taken with Pete. Later, several jurors made the same request. It was pretty extraordinary!

Years later, one of the plaintiff's lawyers wrote an article for a legal publication. He described expert witnesses he encountered and recounted this trial and the role of Pete Conrad. As he acknowledged, the problem was trying to figure out how to cross-examine an astronaut. They couldn't attack him or impeach his credentials. Pete was a hero and extraordinarily well-qualified.

It was fascinating and confirmed my philosophy going forward. I always sought expert witnesses who are highly qualified or unassailable, able to express and defend their opinions and have a powerful "wow" factor like Pete Conrad.

The trial went on for five weeks. When it came to a decision about negligence, the judge directed or told the jury to find that the airline had been negligent, which we admitted from the beginning. The jury then deliberated concerning the issue of punitive conduct and decided in our favor, which was the crucial issue for both sides. Amazingly, even though we won the punitive aspect of the case, we still couldn't settle the cases and started trying compensatory damage cases. We ended up with 11 separate trials before different judges and juries in the same courthouse.

Before each trial, we made large settlement offers, at least what we thought were generous offers to each plaintiff. Every one of them was refused, so I came up with the idea of telling the jury during the opening statement of the damage case, how much we thought the verdict ought to be, and that we would support that number with evidence during the trial. I did that in each of the cases we tried. In each, the jury verdict was either equal to the amount we had suggested or less, which was rather extraordinary.

In the first couple of cases, when I stated in my opening statement what the appropriate award should be, the plaintiff's attorney objected. Each time, the judge ruled in our favor that it was appropriate for the defense to suggest an amount that we believed the evidence would support.

That was the first time a case against an airline went to a jury verdict on a punitive conduct issue. Allowing the punitive conduct issue to be decided by a jury is a precarious proposition for both airlines and insurers. It happened here by virtue of the outrageous demands for punitive damages by the plaintiff's attorneys, which kept the cases from being settled.

US Airways Flight 1016

If you operate an airline, having a plane go down with the loss of life is one of, if not the worst things that can happen. When it happens twice in 28 months, it can't get much worse. Yet, that's what happened precisely to US Airways in the first half of the 1990s. Flight 405 went down at LaGuardia in 1992, and in July of 1994, US Airways Flight 1016 crashed on approach to Columbia, South Carolina.

The Accident

Flight 1016 originated in Charlotte, North Carolina, with bright sunny skies, but as the plane neared the end of the short, 33-minute flight, one of the survivors indicated the sky was almost pitch black with clouds. The short hop between the Carolinas was the fourth leg of a five-leg trip that began in Pittsburgh, with stops in New York City, Charlotte, and Columbia. The final destination was planned to be Memphis, Tennessee. While I was still involved as lead counsel with the crash of Flight 405, US Airways Flight 1016 crashed on approach to landing at Charlotte. Thirty-seven people died, and there were 20 survivors, including both the Captain and the Co-pilot.

The investigation indicated the airplane, a McDonnell Douglas DC-9, slammed into the ground when it encountered a thunderstorm. Although the storm was at the opposite end of the runway from which the plane was approaching to land, the dynamics of the storm created a wind shear, a powerful down-burst, that drove the plane into the ground.

The investigation revealed the pilots were missing im-portant information about the storm as they passed over the airport for the final approach. The had weather reports pre-pared by the National Weather Service broadcast via the Automated Terminal Information Service (ATIS). This report, however, failed to mention any thunderstorms at the Charlotte airport because they had not yet developed. Within minutes of issuing the report, storms began to form. The ATIS put out the next report at 6:36 p.m., and it was broadcast at 6:42, and it did mention thunderstorms and heavy rain at the airport, but that didn't help Flight 1016. Consequently, the pilots never heard a broadcast with a mention of dangerous weather.

US Airways brought a lawsuit against the Federal Government with the assertion that the FAA air traffic control-lers, who I had spent 15 years defending, failed to pass along the weather information to the flight crew. I was intimately aware of the system and its procedures, something which greatly helped our case. Since the crew didn't have all the information, they were unable to make appropriate judgments that might have allowed them to avoid the crash. At the end of the day, the Government settled with us before the trial. It was a substantial payment, and although in the settlement they denied liability, you don't pay eight figures unless concerned there is a signifi-cant risk of an adverse verdict.

The passenger lawsuits that were filed after the accident were all consolidated in the Federal Court in Columbia, South Carolina. Once again, like the Fight 405 litigation, the plaintiffs wanted punitive damages, and we were largely unsuccessful in settling the cases.

It was not surprising that assertions of negligence were made about both the Captain and First Officer, both of whom survived. Ultimately, the Captain went back to flying once the investigation and litigation were finished, and as I write these words, he continues to fly, and we became good friends over the years. Like all tragedies with multiple deaths and injuries, there were dozens of cases. Like the previous crash, the airline and insurers sought to settle them, but once again, the plaintiff's lawyers refused to settle. They wanted values for their cases that went beyond any reasonable compensatory damages.

The Trial

Their strategy for punishing the airline was obvious throughout the depositions and discovery process. They sought to prove that US Airways didn't properly train its pilots regarding how to operate in the vicinity of thunderstorms. According to plaintiffs, allowing these untrained pilots to fly in such situations rose to the level of punitive conduct. This is the conduct they wanted punished and ultimately reflected in the awards. Once again, just like the Flight 405 case, we were unable to settle cases, and we were going to trial.

Frankly, in this particular case, the plaintiff's lawyers were a lot more aggressive than they had been in the Flight 405 litigation. It became apparent that unless the airline and their insurers were prepared to overpay grossly, the cases would have to be tried, at least on the punitive matter.

Since we were once again confronted with having to move forward, I began to think about experts. The airline has a lot at stake, and when these cases go to trial, there's a lot of publicity. This is particularly true when it's asserted that the airline's conduct rose to the point of being punishable. Their reputation, as well as a lot of money, was at stake.

Things worked out well with Pete Conrad in the previous case, and he reinforced what I had thought about the value of a "wow" factor. In this case, the whole fabric of the airline was being attacked in terms of how they trained pilots and conducted operations. I needed to replicate what happened in Cleveland.

Columbia, South Carolina, is located near Shaw Air Force Base. That's where I started looking for experts. I read in the newspapers that General Charles Horner, the Commanding General of the 9th Air Force, who was also the Commander of the air war during Operation Desert Storm, had recently retired. I also knew that US Airways had previously hired a retired Air Force General to assume a senior position in their flight operations department, so I called General Robert Oaks, the relatively new Senior Vice-President of the airline, and explained my plan to have a *superstar* witness. Obviously, I couldn't use him, since he worked for the airline and would be characterized as being prejudiced, but I asked if he knew General Horner, the retiring Commanding General of the 9th Air Force at Shaw Air Base.

General Horner had been the commanding General of the Allied Air War components during Desert Storm. Because of the frequent briefings on TV, he was well-known by the American public. Along with General Norman Schwarzkopf, he was the leader of our forces as our military quickly took back the oil fields from Iraq in Kuwait from the invading Iranians.

General Horner certainly acquitted himself as a hero. He was an F-16 pilot before serving as the Commanding General of the 9th Air Force. Early in the process, with General Oaks vouching for me, I was able to have a phone conversation with General Horner. At that time, he was doing a lot of consulting on behalf of defense manufacturers, particularly those involved with selling military aircraft to Mideast countries. He had dealt with many of these countries during Desert Storm and had a good reputation with them. During one of the trips to Washington, we were able to sit down and talk.

I explained that I might be interested in retaining him on behalf of US Airways to basically do an audit of the airline from the operational and safety perspective. I also chatted with him about his comfort level, as well as his confidence in testifying. These issues are important because anytime you're a witness in a case, your credibility is thrown into question. After he indicated that he was quite comfortable, I told him he would have the run of the company, could talk with anybody, fly on the planes, sit in on classes, talk to management, or whatever else he needed to do to make an accurate assessment. He would be making judgments regarding the level of operations, not unlike what he had done while commanding the 9th Air Force.

Not only did I expect the General to be a witness like Pete Conrad, an American hero, but the trial was going to be in Columbia, South Carolina, just up the road from Shaw Air Force Base where he had served as the Commander. We had a superstar in General Horner with impeccable credentials, and it would be virtually impossible to cross-examine him without calling into question his credibility. In addition, he was a local hero, known by the community of Columbia.

During the trial, when I announced that General Horner would testify the next day, the local newspaper printed the story. The story ran on the front page, and when I arrived at the courthouse, the courtroom was filled to capacity. It's not unusual when a trial begins to have a lot of people in the courtroom, but as the days go by unless it's a high-profile criminal case, typically, the number of spectators drops precipitously. We were several weeks into the trial, and the courtroom was packed because General Horner was perceived as a local hero. It was electric in the room.

In great detail, he described his career and what he did to prepare to give testimony. When he offered his opinions, they came across with a thousand percent credibility, and it was virtually impossible for anybody to challenge this American hero on cross-examination. That's not to say that these plaintiff's lawyers didn't try. It was pretty amazing.

When you get to the level of Four-Star General, Commander of the 9th Air Force, and Desert Storm Commander, you had testified before hostile congressional members, dealt with White House representatives and other powerful individuals, handling a cross-examination by a lawyer is not a problem. The plaintiff's lawyers' approach was a mistake. It came across as trying to question his credibility, and it angered the jurors. General Horner's polish and perfection was evident, not just in his thinking but in the way he expressed himself.

This was the same problem as in the previous trial when lawyers tried to call into question the credibility of a man who had walked on the moon.

When the trial wrapped up for the day, people were milling around the courtroom, still filled with spectators. One gentleman stood out and caught my attention. He was probably in his 30s, perhaps late 20s, and he was sheepishly looking at the General but hesitated to approach him. Many were shaking the General's hand and thanking him for his service to the country. When the crowd thinned out, the young man approached the General, and I overheard the conversation. It was along the lines of being honored to meet the General and that he served during Desert Storm. It was clear that he had been in the Air Force, but I don't think he was a pilot. He perceived that he was in the presence of greatness, and they talked with very low voices to one another throughout the conversation that lasted about two minutes.

The General, who didn't let go after grasping his hand for the handshake, leaned over and embraced the young fellow. The only distinct words I could hear was, "God bless you."

As the young man walked away, I saw tears well up in his eyes. It was a pretty remarkable moment. It reaffirmed the fact that as a trial lawyer utilizing superstars with impeccable, unassailable credentials pays off in extraordinary ways.

The end result of this case was much like the previous US Airways case. Like before, during the opening statement, I told the jury they should, in fact, award compensatory damages because the contract had been breached when the passengers were not delivered from point A to point B safety. They were entitled to compensatory damages, but there was nothing to punish. The judge instructed the jury when giving instructions, reminded them that we had acknowledged the airline's responsibility for compensatory damages and that they should find

we were negligent and return a finding in favor of compensatory damages.

The judge also reminded them that we denied any punitive conduct or entitlement for punitive damages. After delib-
erations, the jury came back with findings consistent with the
judge's instructions and the position we had taken throughout
the trial. Namely that there was nothing to punish.

When the verdict came in, one of the plaintiff's lawyers
started crying, and they weren't tears of joy. They were tears of
disappointment. He had personally invested himself so much
in punishing this airline that it became a personal crusade.
When lawyers take on a personal agenda, they do their clients
a disservice. This is particularly true when somebody's been
injured, or a loved one has been lost in an accident. They are
often not in the best position to make objective decisions. When
the lawyer has an agenda such as I'm going to punish these bad
guys, that plan gets sold to the clients and might not be in their
best interest.

A lawyer's job is to be the very best advocate they can be
on behalf of the client. To do that, they must be able to explain
to the client the pros and cons, the ups and downs, of each decision. In this case, that did not occur because some of the lawyers
had their own emotionally driven agenda.

Dr. Phil Before Dr. Phil

I knew Dr. Phil before there was a Dr. Phil. Just hearing his first name, you know I'm talking about Dr. Phil McGraw of television fame. I first met Dr. Phil while working on the accident in Charlotte, North Carolina, involving US Airways Flight 1016.

Historically, lawyers for both plaintiffs and defendants frequently hire trial consultants. It always depends on the type of case and other unique circumstances. Consultants do a variety of things, including holding mock jury trials before the real trial to determine strategies and the effect witnesses will have on jurors, as well as assisting in jury selection.

It has created an entire sub-industry within the legal profession. These jury consultants, frequently psychologists, may help witnesses prepare to give their testimony, or help lawyers craft an opening statement and closing arguments. At the trial, they might sit in the courtroom and assist with jury selection, profiling the kind of juror wanted based on being the plaintiff or defendant, and the kind of juror who might be more favorable to their case and receptive to various arguments.

The process involves demographic research and other types of information. We've seen movies about jury selection, and often jury psychologists are featured in these movies. Sometimes it's portrayed rather dark and evil regarding the use of psychologists in jury selection.

I've worked with jury psychologists my entire career, and I recall a point in the US Airways Flight 1016 litigation where I started talking with the insurer as well as the client, the airline, about retaining a jury consultant. I explained how they would assist in crafting arguments as well as the valuable resource a jury psychologist provides.

This case followed the Cleveland crash, where we had to try more than a dozen damage cases after winning the decision about punitive damages. We were convinced that we would have to do the same thing in Columbia, South Carolina. With the planning in mind, the issue of a jury consultant was addressed early, and one of the names was a Texas company, *Courtroom Sciences*. The principal of that company was Dr. Phillip McGraw.

This was before Phil came into prominence. That occurred when he was hired by lawyers defending Oprah Winfrey in a Texas case involving beef producers. Winfrey was being sued and hired Phil to assist them in jury selection. That case led to his transition from being Dr. Phillip McGraw, jury consultant with Courtroom Sciences Inc., to Dr. Phil, first on Oprah's show and then on his own national show.

When his name came up with our team, I spoke with him on the phone, and later met him in person. He was retained to assist us with jury and witness issues in the Charlotte accident. We did a focus group because we assumed we were going to be required to try all the cases once again. I traveled to his offices in Dallas, not far from the DFW Airport. It was a beautiful facility, complete with a courtroom. It was all electronically wired. He had jury meeting rooms where you could observe the mock jury through one-way mirrors, and everything was recorded. It was a sophisticated setup. I was struck by how good and easy he was to work within this setting.

The Captain of Flight 1016 survived and ultimately testified at trial. Phil was invaluable in helping him get ready for trial and building his confidence. He also assisted me in creating themes that struck chords with the jury. He was present at jury selection. During the trial, he sat in the audience, and during recesses, based on what he learned regarding the jury during *voir dire*, he provided comments and thoughts about the jurors.

Phil worked with me on the opening statement. This was the case when we admitted the plaintiff should receive compensatory damages and acknowledged the defendant's responsibility to pay those damages. Still, we vociferously denied any punitive conduct or intentional conduct causing the accident. The jury agreed with us.

Phil McGraw was an instrumental part of the trial team, and I must confess that as I sit here today thinking about all the jury consultants I have worked with over the years, he was clearly the most effective. It's not surprising that he was able to transition from Dr. Phil McGraw, jury consultant, to Dr. Phil, television star, easily. He's simply talking to a much bigger jury and bigger audience, but still talking to them directly. He is effective at that. The media and the public's gain of Dr. Phil is the legal profession's loss of Dr. Phillip McGraw.

The Pilot

One of the most surprising things about the crash of US Airways 1016 was the survival of both the Captain and Co-Pilot. Mike Greenlee was the Captain. For Mike, getting over the physical injuries was much easier than the emotional injuries. Early in my representation, I began working with Mike in connection with his anticipated testimony before the National Transportation Safety Board.

The NTSB is an independent agency created by Congress to investigate all transportation accidents. These accidents include aviation, maritime, highway, trucking drones, bus, and rail. They even investigate pipeline explosions, since pipelines are viewed as a means of interstate transportation of gas and oil, so the NTSB holds hearings when there is an explosion. With every accident they investigate, there is a field investigation and sometimes a public factual hearing.

In some ways, it's like a trial, but not adversarial. There are, theoretically, no winners and losers. They don't seek to place liability but to determine probable cause. In the case of an airplane crash, as you would expect, they want to hear from the pilot and co-pilot if they survive. They wanted to interview Mike, so we worked to prepare his testimony, and he did a really fine job. The hearings are public in the sense that they are open to the public and recorded by a court reporter.

Mike was a native Midwesterner living in Ohio. He had been in the Air Force, active duty, and at the time I met him when he was flying for US Airways, he was still flying in the Air Force Reserves, the F-16 fighter. I've commented to several people over the years that if you had walked into a room filled with people and asked to pick out the F-16 pilot, you would immediately locate Mike. He looks like a fighter pilot.

Through the entire process, Mike was very easy to work with and did a fine job of acquitting himself and the company. He clearly and accurately explained his judgments and actions. This was one of those all-too-rare airline accidents with surviving crew members, so investigators did not have to rely solely on the recordings in the *black box*.

We were fortunate to have Captain Greenlee since he was so well-spoken and came across as honest and forthright. Although Mike was not flying, he was working in one of the operational departments at US Airways at the time. He kept his flight status, which required being checked out and going through continuing training.

When we got to the trial, I discussed our strategy with him. I advised him that I was working with the company and his colleagues, and the plan was to acknowledge responsibility and tell the jury that a mistake was made, and some judgments should have been made differently, but he would have the opportunity to explain his thoughts and actions. We talked until I felt he was comfortable with this approach.

Both Captain Greenlee and First Officer Phil Hayes were deposed, and they both did a good job. It was clear that Phil, right after the accident continuing through the investigation, was more emotionally shaken by the accident. We did not plan to call him as a witness, but it was a surprise when the plaintiffs did not call him to testify. I told the jury they were going to hear from Captain Greenlee, and I wanted Mike to understand that we were not going to defend all his judgments. Pilots make instantaneous split-second decisions based on available information. Ninety-nine percent of those judgments are fine, and everything goes as it should. But, sometimes they don't turn out as expected, but that doesn't suggest a deliberate action that requires punitive damages.

I told Mike that when I questioned him in front of the jury, I was going to ask him, "How did it feel to be the Captain, the pilot in command of an airplane full of fare-paying passengers which crashed, resulting in numerous people dead or being injured?"

He gave one of the most heartfelt, honest, forthright responses I've heard. He explained how it weighs on him every day, every minute of his life, and that it will define his life for as long as he's on this Earth. He spoke honestly and emotionally. It wasn't something you can prepare or rehearse. At the end of the day, when you get into a courtroom, and you're a witness, no matter how much preparation you've had, there is no way to be ready to answer a question like this. This is especially true when there are lawyers and people pointing at you as the one who made the wrong judgment, causing lives to be lost. No amount of preparation is enough.

When it came time for closing arguments, this is how I described the pilot's actions. *"Now, Mr. Rapoport and Mr. Moller have told you that their clients have proven not only negligence but that their clients are also entitled to punitive damages. Now, at the outset before I say anything else to you I want to tell you there is nothing whatever to punish here. By any definition, by any measure through the expression of any words what occurred on July 2nd is a tragedy. Good people lost their lives, or were injured but you can't undo it and I can't undo it. There is no way to undo what occurred.*

"Michael Greenlee who is sitting in the front row has to wake up every morning. Jennifer Greenlee has to wake up every morning and go to sleep every night knowing that he was the pilot of that aircraft. He made it clear to you in no uncertain terms that irrespective of what you do in the context of the legal system that he holds himself responsible for what occurred. That he asked himself harder questions than any of the lawyers could even ask him. He has to live with that the rest of his life. There is nothing to punish here. Nobody, whether it is US Airways, Michael Greenlee, nobody knowingly, willfully, wantonly or with the complete absence of care, flew into a thunderstorm.

After you strip away all the words, after you strip away all the arguments, there is only one question left in this whole case. Did captain Michael Greenlee, a man who has been flying his whole life, his whole life, knowingly fly into a thunderstorm on July 2nd."

Mike was honest with himself, and the jury saw that he was also honest with them. He did acknowledge fault. He admitted to breaching the contract of passage, but Mike, along with General Horner, went a long way toward defusing any anger on the part of the jury directed to US Airways. Anger is precisely what the plaintiff's attorneys wanted because anger translates into punitive damages.

"And the final witness we presented was general Charles Horner, now there's a man, if you look up the word Integrity, if you look up the word competence, if you look up the word honesty in the dictionary, you will very likely find his picture. Here's a man who calls things the way he sees them and he doesn't care where the chips fall. Here's a man who was examined by Mr. Rapoport at length about how much he was being paid, and then was criticized during that questioning because he didn't know.

"Now, I find it interesting that the concept of coming to court and telling the truth for truth's sake should be so surprising. Remember the deposition excerpt that Mr. Rapoport read to you-- to General Horner and i asked that the last question and answer be read, and General Horner stated in that deposition, when asked about what he was being paid and he said he really didn't know because he didn't know you got paid for telling the truth.

"Quite frankly, I find it somewhat surprising, I suppose I could use the word insulting, to insinuate that that man, that that hero could do anything but tell the truth. What did he tell us? He was asked to examine US Airways top to bottom. Well, how did he get involved? His colleague, his former colleague, General Robert Oaks, said, "Can you help me?" These gentlemen come from a world where when one of them **asks** *the other to do something, they do it. These gentlemen don't understand that kind of world. He was asked to go in and find if everything or anything that Mr. Burnett and Captain Clyne* (plaintiff's experts) *said was true or untrue. And to accomplish that task, he read everything, he talked to people, he flew on airplanes, he asked hard questions and then when he got answers, he looked behind the answers. Because whether he was General Charles Horner commanding the air war over desert storm or he was General Charles Horner looking at US Airways.*

"He was still General Charles Horner and he only knew one way to do things. Think about it, here's a man who represents the highest ideals of credibility throughout the world, he's decorated and honored by governments throughout the world, and plaintiffs' counsel would suggest in their questioning that he's biased or he's driven by his fee. Do you really think that General Charles Horner is going to come here for money? Do you really think he's going to come here because he thinks he's going to get a job with US Airways?

"The reason he came here is because somebody asked him to do them a favor, that's the kind of world these gentlemen live in. Now, what he found was a company which didn't only give lip service to safety but he found a company where safety was the number one priority, that it practiced it, that preached it, that practiced it at every single level. Now, what qualified an Air Force General, a man who is not a DC-9 pilot, who's never worked for an airline, who's never flown a DC-9, to do these things? And I can't help but make an observation at this point, there are paid experts and then there are experts who get compensated for their time. Paid experts who get paid for their testimony, 800-hour exercise in hindsight, versus people like Mr. Conrad and General Horner who appear before you to tell the truth and do get compensated for their time.

"Mr. Rapoport talks about the astronaut and the general as if those are dirty words, that those are dirty words. Could we have gone out and hired paid experts? Sure, we could have done that, absolutely, they advertise in all the legal journals. But what we were interested in was getting people in here who first and foremost could present you with integrity, with truth, with honesty beyond reproach. Mr. Conrad and General Horner have spent their entire careers not only protecting our way of life but advancing the ideals of the very system that allow us to be here. For this, Mr. Rapoport refers to them as the astronaut and the general as if those are some sort of demeaning terms. Well, we should be ashamed.

*"You heard my final question to General Horner, it **was,** if he had found anything unsafe at US Airways, would he have told you, and his answer was not only would he have told you but he would have told the FAA. You didn't hear a single word from Captain Clyne in all the deposition testimony and all the trial testimony, over the 800 hours of his work, despite his condemnation of US Airways at*

every level, the only thing he didn't condemn was our food service and it's probably the thing that deserves the most condemnation, the food is lousy, despite his condemnation of management, of pilots, of procedures, that he had ever reported anything to the FAA or that the thought had even entered his mind.

"He's dedicated his whole life to the very things that he sat up there and told you about. to suggest that he's not qualified to tell us whether an aviation operation like US Airways has the right priorities, has the right procedures, or carries them out at all levels, is disingenuous, to suggest that anything, including money, can shape his opinions is to ignore who we are talking about."

US Airways Flight 427: Bad Luck Comes in Threes

A s hard as it might be to believe, after two tragic crashes in two years, things got even worse for US Airways. On September 8, 1994, sixty-eight days after the crash of Flight 1016, US Airways Flight 427 nose-dived into the ground outside of Hopewell Township near Pittsburgh, Pennsylvania.

The Crash

The flight originated at O'Hare International Airport in Chicago with a final destination scheduled for West Palm Beach, Florida. In between was a planned stop in Pittsburgh. All the passengers and crew members were killed when the plane exploded after striking the ground at 300 miles per hour. The 132 fatalities were the second largest number of deaths in US Airways crash.

The aircraft was a Boeing 737-3B7 that had been in service for seven years, recording more than 18,000 hours of flight time. US Airways hired captain Peter Germano in 1981, and the First Officer, Chuck Emmett, was brought on board in 1987. Both men were considered experienced, highly skilled, and excellent pilots. Their qualifications played an important role in the NTSB investigation of the crash.

It was a clear, late summer evening as they approached the Pittsburgh airport, Flight 427 was positioned behind Delta Airlines Flight 1083, a Boeing 727. This was also an important consideration during the follow-up investigation. The flight encountered wake turbulence, sort of horizontal vortices coming off the Delta flight, and there were three sudden thumps. On the flight recorder, it sounded like clicking sounds and then a louder thump. At that moment, the plane began a sharp bank and then a roll to the left. At 6,000 feet in the air, it was obvious they were in trouble.

The recording reveals that Captain Germano shouted out, "Hold on!" numerous times.

Hearing the physical exertion in his voice, Emmet simply said, "Oh shit!"

Germano replied, "What the hell is this?" as air traffic control noticed the plane was descending without permission.

"Four-twenty-seven emergency!" hollered Captain Germano into the keyed microphone.

The mic stayed on for the remainder of the event as the plane pitched nose down toward the ground. A few other frightened exclamations were recorded as the plane plunged nose down into the ground at high speed. All of this happened within 28 seconds after the encounter with the wake turbulence.

The Investigation

The NTSB investigation was difficult. All 127 passengers and five crew members were killed, but 2,000 body bags were required to contain 6,000 human remains. You can imagine how difficult the identification was for the coroner. It also took a long time to piece together the evidence necessary to determine the cause of the crash.

Although the plane did encounter wake turbulence, it was determined it would not have been sufficient alone to cause the head first crash. The abrupt nature of the change just before the dive immediately suggested to the investigators that the rudder was the problem. At that point, they needed to determine if it moved because of a malfunction or by pilot command. As you can imagine, this decision was crucial to the resolution of the trial case.

Flight recordings were scrutinized, not only for statements but also for breathing patterns and sounds. It was apparent the pilots were fighting for control of the plane, but again, the issue remained was it a malfunction or was the wrong rudder pedal stomped in excitement over the wake turbulence?

As a testament to the difficulty of the investigation, the NTSB didn't present their conclusions until 1999, five years after the accident. The probable cause was determined to be a problem with the rudder that makes the plane rotate on its vertical axis. Somehow, the crew lost control of the rudder. The report stated, "The rudder surface most likely deflected in a direction opposite to that commanded by the pilots as a result of a jam of the main rudder power control unit…" The report noted similar rudder problems in two previous Boeing 737 crashes.

At the time of the crash, it was the seventh-deadliest aviation disaster in the history of the U.S. It was also the fifth crash in the period starting from 1989 to 1994. As a result of the problem with the rudder, US Airways agreed that pilots would receive training on how to deal with this potential situation.

Although Boeing maintained that the co-pilot inadvertently sent the rudder in the wrong direction while in panic and for some unknown reason maintained that position until impact, the aircraft maker did agree to redesign the rudder control system with a redundant backup.

Preparations for Trial

From the beginning, I was involved with assisting the company through the NTSB hearings on the Pittsburgh accident of Flight 427. At that time, the NTSB typically held their hearings in the city nearest to or where the accident occurred. The practice was to rent a ballroom in a hotel, and since it was a local accident, they prepared for heavy media coverage, both local and national.

Since it was an airline accident, family members and friends were also in attendance. Additionally, to compound matters, Pittsburgh was a center of its US Airways's operations, where they had their maintenance department, and it was one of their hubs. The hearings were heavily publicized, well-covered, and attended.

One of the things I started to think about from the beginning was who would be a good candidate to serve as an expert for this case, much like with the Flight 405 and Flight 1016 accidents. Pete Conrad and General Chuck Horner were excellent choices, and at this time, I was still involved in those litigations. However, even though I knew that any trial in the Pittsburgh accident would be a long time coming, I didn't want to wait. There is always a plaintiff's lawyer who shows up days after an accident to grab the headlines. Plaintiff lawyers want to be the first to file a lawsuit. The hope is that when families notice the first lawsuit has already been filed, they will jump on board and use the same lawyer, even though they have no idea what caused the accident. It allows early lawyers to secure more clients.

In December of 1988, Pan Am Flight 103 blew up over Scotland, killing 259 people. There was an open solicitation of cases by plaintiff lawyers after the crash. Lawyers reached out to grieving families making numerous promises to them. They sent out videotapes promoting themselves and their services. It became horrific for a family grieving the loss of a loved one. It was tantamount to a lawyer following an ambulance to the hospital.

Some plaintiff lawyers, in signing up clients, agreed to work on a reduced contingency agreement, and even prepared to pay advance funds to the prospective client to induce them to "sign on the dotted line." In other words, they would give the prospective client a check against the inevitable recovery amount that will eventually be awarded. It's not a question of "if" they get the money, they're going to get money; it's only a matter of how much. When the plaintiff's lawyer advances $5,000 or $25,000, it's essentially a sure bet for them.

Since I knew the lawyers would be aggressive, I started thinking about who my expert would be. By this time, Pete Conrad and I had become good friends. He was looking at doing a lot of consulting, not necessarily in the field of airplane accidents, but commercial space exploration. If you think about where we are today with Virgin Galactic and Space X and other commercial activities in space, Pete Conrad would be at the forefront if he had survived.

The story of his death is a sad one. I remember getting dressed in the morning, and the news was playing in the background. There was an announcement that Pete Conrad, the Apollo 12 astronaut, had died following a motorcycle accident. I immediately made contact with Nancy, his wife, on the phone. Pete had been on a motorcycle ride outside Ojai, California, on a dirt road. His big Harley Davidson went out from under him when he hit a depression or a rut of some kind, and he flew off his bike. He was wearing a helmet and conscious when his riding partner called 911.

He was unconscious by the time he reached the emergency room in Ojai. They rushed him into emergency surgery, but he didn't make it. I do not doubt that Pete Conrad would have been at the forefront of the commercialization of space. He had a private satellite company already in the works, and he was already thinking far ahead of anyone else at the time.

Pete and I were always extremely upfront with one another. A couple of weeks before his death, I was in California assisting with a personal legal matter for Nancy's son. Pete was traveling, and as I recall, I spent the night at Pete's home. As Nancy and I were leaving, I saw this big Harley Davidson in the garage, and I asked if that was Pete's, and she said, "Yea," and I just sort of shook my head.

But back to the Pittsburgh accident…

When I called Pete about the Pittsburgh crash, I said, "I need the next Pete Conrad."

He had already testified twice, and I didn't want him in a position where his credibility or objectiveness would ever be questioned by being viewed as a professional expert witness.

Pete proceeded to tell me about Hoot Gibson. Robert L. "Hoot" Gibson was in the process of retiring from NASA. Aviation was a natural field for him. His mother was the first female U.S. Mail pilot, and he speaks of his parents telling him that when he was a baby, they would take him on the airplane and put him on the floor of the cockpit when they took a trip. He served in the Navy as a fighter pilot.

Along with a degree in aerodynamics, he has designed his own airplane. He has been flying in the Reno Air Races for decades, where, a few years ago, he became the Unlimited Class Champion.

Like many astronauts, Hoot moved from the Navy to NASA and was involved in five missions, including several as the Commander. He ultimately became the Chief Astronaut and ultimately retired from the government. His wife was another astronaut, Dr. Rhea Sheddon. She had also flown in the Space Shuttle, serving as a mission specialist surgeon. It's a remarkable family!

An amazing thing about Hoot is that when he retired from NASA, he went to work as a First Officer for Southwest Airlines. The First Officer sits on the right side of the cockpit with the Captain in the left seat. Obviously, the Captain is in charge of the crew, including the First Officer sitting on the right-side. Imagine what it was like on that first flight when the Captain met the new first officer sitting at his side. This new co-pilot just completed his training and initial checkouts and has no time as a commercial airline pilot. Yet, he has flown in the Reno Air Races for years, flown on the Space Shuttle as Commander, served as the chief astronaut, served as a naval fighter pilot, and has an aerodynamics degree. In spite of all that, I would describe Hoot as an "aw-shucks" kind of guy.

I'm confident that Hoot would have deliberately set out to make that cockpit as comfortable as possible. He worked for Southwest until FAA age restrictions forced him to retire at age 60 since raised to age 65. I have no doubt he would have flown for another five years if allowed when he retired. When I contacted him through Pete Conrad's introduction, he was preparing to leave the airline.

He was the youngest 60-year-old I've ever met, filled with boundless enthusiasm. Two summers ago, my wife and I went to the wedding of his daughter, where, after he got an Internet "ordination," he presided while wearing his Navy dress whites.

When we talked, I explained everything to Hoot, and fortunately, I had Pete Conrad vouching for me. I had found the "next Pete Conrad" in terms of working with airlines, and I retained him to testify in the event we had a trial arising out of Flight 427.

Lawsuits

The assertions against US Airways filed on behalf of the families of the victims were unusual because of the inconsistent theories about the crash. The Boeing Company was sued, as well as Parker Hannifin, the manufacturer of the components of the rudder assembly. From the passenger's perspective, the assertion was that the airplane had been improperly designed so that when the pilot pressed the right rudder pedal, instead of going right, it went left. It was basically a design error, and there was nothing the pilot could have done.

The position of Boeing and Parker Hannifin was the accident was caused by pilot error. When the plane encountered turbulence, it caused the pilots to react improperly and stall the airplane. In aviation terminology, stalling does not mean the engine stopped running but that the wings stopped producing lift. In effect, they were saying the pilots panicked and reacted improperly, and for 23 seconds, didn't do anything other than panic and watch the airplane corkscrew into the ground.

On behalf of the airline, our position was that this theory was foolish. To suggest that two highly experienced pilots would have been panicked by encountering turbulence that would have been little more than a bump was incorrect. It was irrational that these two experienced pilots would feel a bump and then do nothing to resolve any problems. The NTSB was very thorough and uncovered two previous crashes that were likely caused by the same design failure with the rudder pedal.

All the cases were filed in Pennsylvania Federal Court and consolidated into a single liability trial. Representing US Airwaysways and their insurers because of the contract of passage, we settled every passenger case. The message we had delivered in Flight 405 and Flight 1016 cases had finally been heard by the aviation plaintiff's bar that if you press US Airways, they will go to trial. We had done it on Flight 405 and Flight 1016. I think it took those two catastrophes and trials to verdict to make our position clear. We had acknowledged responsibility for compensatory damages but would not pay unreasonable amounts of punitive damages. They finally understood that we would settle cases fairly and reasonably but would not be bullied into excessive settlements.

Once all the passenger suits had been settled, what remained was Boeing, US Airways, and Parker Hannifin pointing the finger at one another. This was a delicate situation because all three of these companies relied on business with one another. US Airways flew Boeing planes, and Boeing needed Parker Hannifin parts. This relationship transcended a single accident and needed to continue for everyone's sake.

Boeing and its insurers agreed to settle with US Airways for a very substantial percentage of everything the airline had paid. That left us, on behalf of US Airways, with Parker Hannifin, and we strongly believed we had developed sufficient evidence that Parker Hannifin's design was flawed, causing the rudder to sporadically jam and then spontaneously release, except in our case, it did not release. Despite our evidence, Parker Hannifin would not settle. They continued to insist that the cause of the crash was pilot error, so we went to trial in Federal Court in Pittsburgh.

Hitting turbulence for an experienced pilot is like hitting a speed bump on the street. It might jolt you for a second, but then it's over. It doesn't put you in a panic state and cause you to input the wrong controls for 23 seconds as your airplane dives into the ground. There was nothing on the recording recovered from the black box that supported their theory. Parker Hannifin called an expert witness with thousands of hours in the cockpit. However, being highly experienced flying a plane doesn't necessarily relate to courtroom savvy or the ability to communicate with a jury. He was highly susceptible to a searching cross-examination and looking back, I think I made the most of the cross-examination.

As the plaintiffs seeking to recover in this case, we went first. As I had learned to do previously, when it was time for Hoot Gibson to take the stand, I asked, "Have you ever gone to space? Have you ever commanded the space shuttle? Have you ever been on the International Space Station? Have you ever flown in the Reno Air Races?

Hoot acquitted himself very well and communicated that there was no question he couldn't answer. He understood what the case was about and the injustice of blaming the pilots. The jury heard him clearly. I can't think of a time since that point where I've encountered a witness with the qualifications that make him a superstar and also with the ability to communicate that expertise, common-sense, and highly technical information in such a plain-spoken fashion. Watching the defense lawyer trying to cross-examine this guy was the height of pure entertainment. It was almost to the point of embarrassment, and me feeling bad for my opponent… but not quite.

The jury was only asked to allocate fault for the accident. Remember, US Airways had already paid one hundred percent of the passenger claims. The jury's job was to simply determine the percentage of fault for each of the three parties – US Airways, Parker Hannifin, and Boeing. By including Boeing, even though they had settled with us, Parker Hannifin was hoping to dilute their percentage of the fault. The jury findings were zero fault to US Airways, 75% to Parker Hannifin, and 25% to Boeing. This was a major loss for Parker Hannifin.

That meant that they were responsible for paying to US Airways, 75% of all of the settlements, including the value of the airplane itself that had been paid by the insurers to US Airways. Now the thing that is so interesting about that is when you added up the 75% that Parker Hannifin had to pay to US Airways, the amount of money that Boeing had already paid to US Airways, the airline and its insurers actually recovered in excess of a hundred percent of everything that it had paid. The verdict was never appealed, and to my knowledge, it's the only time that an airline has recovered over a hundred percent of the money that it had to pay following a catastrophic accident. It was an extraordinary result that obviously everybody on the US Airways and their insurer side was happy about, and to my knowledge, has never occurred again.

Hoot Gibson "blames" me for turning him into a consultant. By far, he is the best witness in a courtroom I have ever dealt with in my 50 years of being an aviation litigator. Hoot and his wife Rhea remain close friends, and has Hoot continued his career as an aviation consultant/expert. The best in the business!

The Reno Air Races: Dealing With the Next Crisis

Since 1964, each September at Reno Stead Airport located a few miles north of Reno, Nevada, the "world's fastest motorsport" happens. The multi-day event features airplane races in six classifications and airshow-type demonstrations.

The first races were organized by war veteran Bill Stead and were held at Sky Ranch airfield, a dirt airstrip generously measured as 2,000 feet long. A couple of years later, nearby Stead Air Force base was closed, and the races have been held at that location since.

The most anticipated classification is the Unlimited class, featuring modified and stock World War II and Korean fighters. The planes fly at an altitude of 50 to 100 feet at speeds of hundreds of miles an hour. It's quite an event to witness, something that I think every aviation enthusiast ought to see at least once in life.

The fans are passionate, and who can blame them. Watching souped-up vintage warplanes speeding around a tight eight-mile oval track at 500 miles per hour and only 50 feet above the ground is an impressive sight. In each of the last ten years, the event has welcomed 200,000 visitors and contributed more than $80 million to the economy.

This type of racing was popular in the 1930s and 40s with the big race event held in Cleveland, Ohio. In 1949, pilot Bill Odom lost control of his plane during the headline event and crashed into a house near the course. The pilot, along with a mother and infant on the ground were killed. As a result, the races were shut down for the next 15 years until Bill Stead came along.

By the year 2011, the event had become an annual staple for airplane enthusiasts as they flocked to Reno. However, 2011 also became a watershed year for the Reno Air Races because of a well-publicized tragic accident. The mishap occurred when a modified P-51 aircraft named *Galloping Ghost* sped around the course at a speed of 445 knots (513 mph), faster than it had ever flown before at the races, shot up into the sky, causing the 17 Gs of acceleration to incapacitate the pilot. As the plane uncontrollably rolled over, it slammed into a box seating area on the ground filled with fans and showered debris for hundreds of yards. The initial NTSB report described it like this: "The airplane descended in an extremely nose-low attitude and collided with the ground in the box seat area near the center of the grandstand seating area."

The pilot, James K. "Jimmy" Leeward, was killed along with ten others on the ground. Sixty-nine others suffered various levels of injury from the scattering wreckage. Fortunately, the plane hit the ground near the edge of the crowd rather than the center, which would have resulted in many additional deaths.

The *Galloping Ghost* was a well-known aircraft that competed year after year at the Reno Air Races. The P-51 had been extensively modified over many years since it was first raced in 1946. It had been crashed, repaired, and modified several times and appeared significantly different than the original P-51. Most notably, the wings were ten feet shorter to help increase speed.

Pilots competed in several classifications, including a category for pure jet airplanes. The unlimited class has no limitation on the horsepower of the aircraft, and the *Galloping Ghost* frequently dominated that class.

The pilots who fly these airplanes in the races are highly experienced and focused. They have spent a lot of time in the particular plane they're flying and this type of racing. In order to compete in the Reno Air Races, pilots must attend a special training school as a predicate to everything else. They also have numerous qualifying requirements, and safety has always been a major focus on the races. The pilot of the *Galloping Ghost* was a 74-year-old real estate developer and an experienced race and stunt pilot. Leeward had competed in the Reno Air Races since the 1980s.

This was not the first accident at the Reno races. The nature of the kind of flying that's done there has resulted in accidents over the years. However, the pilots understand the increased risk. They operate at extraordinarily low altitudes at very high speeds, which greatly limits reaction time when a problem arises.

The 2011 crash of the *Galloping Ghost* took on another dimension in that it crashed into spectators resulting in death and injuries.

When I heard about this accident, I was on the east coast in my Virginia home outside Washington. One of the first things I did was to reach out to Hoot Gibson, the astronaut who helped with the US Airways Flight 427 crash. I thought of him because I knew he had a passion for flying in the Reno Air Races and was a fixture in the unlimited class. The classification features an extraordinary collection of World War II and Korean War vintage aircraft that have been restored and meticulously maintained.

My purpose in speaking with Hoot was to connect with somebody in the Reno organization. I wanted to talk with them in terms of potentially assisting the organization through the investigation. Like many organizations and companies, they didn't have a sense of appreciation as to what would occur in the context of an accident investigation of this magnitude with the National Transportation Safety Board.

I also spoke with General Chuck Horner, who I worked with during the Charlotte accident. General Horner had obviously come out of the highest levels of the Air Force and was very close to General Ron Fogelman, who had been the former Chief of Staff of the Air Force and was on the Board for the Reno Air Races organization. As a result, I was able to talk with the Director of the Reno organization that conducts the races.

They retained my services, and I represented and assisted them through the investigation. This included the issues having to do with interviewing various witnesses. Most of them were volunteers because aviation is a passion, and fans want to help. We also helped with interviews with the NTSB and the review of their safety school, including their safety protocols, and assisting them through the whole NTSB process.

One of the most significant and understandable concerns of the Reno Air Races folks is the tremendous impact the event has on the entire community on an annual basis. As we noted earlier, it not only draws people but also tens of millions of dollars every year into the local economy. There was also significant concern on the part of the community, especially the business community. There was, as a result, great interest among the aviation community that there might be a public or political outcry to terminate the races permanently.

Mike Houghton was head of the race organization at the time. I suggested to Mike that he establish an independent blue-ribbon committee or audit team to review safety protocols, crowd management protocols, and the entire operation. Issuing a public report would demonstrate total transparency. The team could also make appropriate recommendations that would address any concerns regarding the viability of future races. It would assure the community of their commitment to safety. Also, because of the level of sponsorship of the races, it would alleviate the nervousness that also occurs after this sort of high-profile accident.

I should also note that the NTSB investigation determined that the pilot of the *Galloping Ghost* was incredibly experienced. It turned out there was a fatigue crack on one of the surfaces of the aircraft resulting in a mechanical failure that caused the accident. The fact that there was a mechanical failure of this type was surprising to me in the context of the Reno Air Races.

In passenger operations, the airplanes are scrutinized seven ways from Sunday, both mechanically and maintenance wise. The fact that you would have a fatigue crack or have a mechanical failure in one of these airplanes at the Reno Air Races is surprising because those airplanes are even more meticulously and microscopically maintained. In any event. It happened.

I should also note that all of the claims, both for personal injury and death, were settled by the insurers for the Reno Air Races. That was another issue that concerned the Reno Air Race folks. There was a fear that they would not be able to secure insurance if they continued the races. Even though the sponsors might stand by them and the community might support them, the question arose, could they get insurance because of this particular accident. This concern went to the heart of the questions that we wanted the audit team to address. This approach appealed to Mike Houghton and other leaders of the organization.

The audit team that I put together included Hoot Gibson, whose credibility was absolutely impeccable, both in the Reno air community and the aviation community as a whole. The team also included a former senior safety official from the FAA and another Reno Air Race participant and former champion. Each had unassailable credibility and brought the highest level of expertise to the task.

The audit team completed a series of interviews and reviews, as well as a historical look at the history of the races. The result was a report presented to the Board of Directors that addressed, among other things, the safety procedures during the race. Everything they did was transparent, and the race folks held a press conference presenting the team's findings.

It was clear that the audit team was independent and operated with great concern for safety. The caliber of people like Hoot Gibson and others on the audit team made this clear. The Reno Air Race organization did not even receive an advance copy of the report prior to the press conference, and other than making its personnel available for interviews had no input into the report itself.

The key to successful management of a crisis is to get out in front of the situation, understanding the potential consequences. This is important in all situations in the world of civil litigation. Having experience in dealing with a crisis is invaluable in understanding potential consequences. If you haven't been there, it's not really possible to comprehend the implications of situations in three to six months. The Reno Air Race folks dealt with this tragedy successfully, and it's evident in the fact that the races went forward in 2012 and have taken place every year since then. (The race in 2020 was canceled because of the pandemic.)

One year after the crash, the NTSB issued seven safety recommendations for future air races. These recommendations included design and layout of the course, specifically moving the course further from the fans. It also spoke of pre-race inspections, airworthiness of modifications on the aircraft, and a few other issues.

There has been and will continue to be accidents or other serious incidents. That's the nature of flying. The 2011 crash was unique because it involved a crowd of spectators and deaths among fans. The way the Reno folks moved forward provides a template for how other organizations and companies ought to operate in the future.

Before the crash of 2011 involving the death of spectators, the Reno Air Races experienced one pilot death every two and a half years from 1964 until 2010. In the years since 2011, only one pilot has died in a crash. While flying will never be 100% safe, the current situation suggests it is possible to preserve the features that make racing exciting while maintaining the highest level of safety.

Feld Entertainment: Big Tops and Big Cats!

Earlier I explained how I *stumbled* into the airline industry, and it's accurate to say that the majority of my legal work has remained in that area. However, I have experience in other arenas that have been equally interesting. One of those fascinating clients is Feld Entertainment.

A partner, working at a previous law firm, had several non-aviation related connections. He had been a Virginia politician at the state level and formed relationships while in office. When he joined my firm, he introduced me to many of those people from the Commonwealth of Virginia. It was one of those contacts who opened the doors for me to be introduced to Feld Entertainment, headquartered at that time in Virginia. Their office was not too far from where I'm currently sitting.

As their name implies, they were in the entertainment business. That includes a number of the Disney Ice Shows all over the world. Feld Entertainment dates back to 1938, when Irvin Feld, the founder of the business, operated a drugstore in Washington, D.C. The store made a good portion of its profit by selling records, which led Feld to open a chain of record stores, and then to become a record producer.

The big breakthrough came for Feld when he devised the concept of holding concerts in large public arenas. He featured entertainers like Frank Sinatra and the Beatles. In 1956, Feld joined the circus. Not as a performer but as a manager and booking agent for Ringling Brothers and Barnum & Bailey Circus. He was successful and ultimately purchased the circus himself in 1967. At the time, the circus was struggling, but Feld turned the fortunes around. He moved the show from the typical outdoor setting to large, indoor arenas. It became a profitable business. One other enterprise owned by Feld Entertainment was the Siegfried and Roy Magic Show in Las Vegas, but we will discover more about them shortly.

My original introduction to Feld Entertainment came after a train derailment. The Ringling Brothers Circus traveled throughout the United States on two trains. They had a Red Unit and a Blue Unit, which were really two separate shows touring in different locations around the country. Although the circus originally traveled by semis and busses, they had long ago switched to trains because of cost and convenience. The circus owned the cars and would hook up a locomotive depending on whose track they used. It might be Amtrak or some other company. Their headquarters were in Sarasota, Florida, and that's where they spent the winter months.

Ringling Brothers had its own major train operation. They bought old Pullman cars and boxcars that had been retired by other railroads. These cars were brought to Florida to be reconditioned and retrofitted for the Red and Blue Unit tours. It was in Florida where the derailment that brought me into the picture occurred.

The accident happened near Lakeland, Florida, about 90 miles to the northeast of Ringling Brothers home. A train of 53 cars carrying 200 performers and circus workers along with 60 animals in the Blue Unit went off the tracks in the mid-morning of January 14, 1994. Fifteen people were injured, and two died in the most serious train accident in the history of the circus.

The two deaths included one of the leading elephant trainers in the world who not only performed in the Center Ring but was also in charge of Ringling's elephant research and breeding facility. The other fatality was a 28-year-old woman from Texas who had worked for the circus for several years as a clown. There are two other interesting facts about this accident. First, there were no animals in any of the 17 cars that derailed. Second, during news coverage of the accident, a television station's helicopter crashed in a nearby field, injuring two members of the news crew. I was not involved in handling that accident.

As always, the NTSB was on the scene quickly to begin their investigation of the derailment. Early indications suggested that a steel wheel on the 22nd car broke apart, but the damaged car traveled for two more miles before hitting a switch, knocking it off the tracks. The NTSB official in charge of the investigation reported that pieces of the wheel were found along the route, and a witness observed it coming apart.

As I previously observed, companies are seldom prepared to handle an NTSB investigation and all the other things that happen following a tragic accident. Many are actually surprised that the NTSB is involved in non-aviation incidents. In fact, the NTSB is even involved when pipeline accidents occur, and they investigate the practices of the energy companies involved. We obviously had the relationships needed to help clients make good decisions. This history is what allowed us to help Ringling Brothers through this accident.

The NTSB is headquartered in Washington, D.C., and most of the investigators operate out of that location, especially on the railroad side. They often involve people who had been with or who have retired from the rail industry and moved over from the Federal Railroad Administration or the NTSB. Suddenly, as a part of the investigation, Ringling Brothers found themselves involved with unfamiliar rules and procedures, as well as regulations about what they, an American institution, could and could not say to the public about the accident. The company was not allowed to conduct their own investigation into an accident. Insurers, who find their clients involved in an NTSB investigation, need to be aware of this, as well.

For example, in this case, there was circus personnel who were killed in the accident. Their families are only allowed to be contacted by the insurer after a fixed period of time. These types of restrictions made it a whole new, and in many respects, a foreign world to insurers. I have spent my entire career operating in that world.

Entering the investigation, Ringling Brothers had the advantage of a stellar record for their privately owned 53-car trains. The trains were required to have a certification that met all federal safety standards, and the NTSB reported that the certification requirements had been met at the time it was issued. The findings pointed to three issues. First, passengers had no way of stopping the train during an emergency. A witness reported seeing people on board looking out the window at the broken wheel, but the system that would have allowed passengers to arbitrarily stop the train had been removed. In fact, the young woman who died was struck down as she made her way to notify the trains operators of the emergency.

The second issue was that Ringling Brothers failed to secure furniture on the train. The woman's death was caused by being crushed by file cabinets moving around as a result of the derailment. The NTSB report indicated that the train did not adhere to standards for securing such items. Finally, the train had brake problems. A metallurgist testified that a stuck brake might have caused the broken wheel. It rubbed, metal to metal, for miles. Responding to these findings, Ringing officials made extensive changes to the train to make it safer.

I found myself with a new, interesting client once I traveled to Florida to see the train operation and the winter home of the circus when they weren't touring. The trains were kept in the same location. Repairs and modifications necessary for outfitting the railroad cars all happened in Florida. The next time the show came to Washington was much more interesting to me after learning the inner workings of this unique business.

I was also able to observe after their performance in Washington how they packed everything for a quick exit to the next location. It has to happen quickly so that they can make it to the next city on time. The whole process is highly choreographed, both in terms of breaking everything down and getting it to the rail yard for travel.

I did learn that railroad accidents are less complicated than most airplane crashes. The work required as a lawyer was much less than what we would do in an airline accident.

My relationship with Feld Entertainment led me to another fascinating client. Given my passion for all things magic since the age of six, I couldn't think of a more perfect client.

Feld also owned the *Siegfried and Roy Magic Show* in Las Vegas. Famed Las Vegas developer Steve Wynn called "them the most successful entertainment attraction in Las Vegas history." They performed before capacity crowds for 30 years, 48 weeks a year. The indispensable element of the successful show was created by the tigers and other exotic animals and the fear they generated for audiences. Tigers and lions roamed freely throughout Siegfried and Roy's massive Las Vegas mansion.

Kenneth Feld, head of Feld Entertainment, explained that their show required a lot of money, "probably the most expensive show, ever, in the history of the world…" On top of that, Siegfried and Roy signed a huge contract worth $57 million over five years, the biggest contract ever signed in Las Vegas at the time.

Their fame centered on the large cats—tigers and lions—that were an integral part of every show. They gave the appearance of being in complete control of the wild animals, but in reality, behind the scenes, there was a trainer for each one. Often, especially the larger ones were tethered to the floor by invisible wires to limit their movement. They were, after all, wild animals.

Tragically, Roy was seriously injured by one of the cats during a performance in 2003. He was never able to perform on a Vegas stage again, and even more tragically, Roy recently passed away.

My introduction came much before the tragedy of Roy's accident. I received a phone call from the general counsel of Feld Entertainment, indicating there was a problem involving one of the cats and a veterinarian who took care of the animals. Immediately, I was obviously *all in* because of my lifelong fascination with magic. It has been my hobby since the age of six or seven, and Siegfried and Roy were the biggest stars in the biggest arena.

Even before the phone call, I had attended their show when I was in Las Vegas on another piece of litigation, not involving Siegfried and Roy. It was a wonderful show as the cats appeared to roam pretty much unrestricted on the stage under the command of the two men, especially Roy. The general counsel called me about a matter that involved a vet giving a vaccination to a white tiger.

Apparently, the tiger was in an isolation cage that restricted movement to little more than pacing back and forth. The purpose of the cages is to allow the vet access to the cat and provide the shot. After giving the shot, the vet was backing out of the small cage, and the cat was startled by something and quickly turned to face the vet. Reflexively, the vet apparently stood up straight and cracked his head on the top of the cage. He tumbled out of the cage, onto the ground about eight inches below the cage. Because his head struck the tile floor, he claimed injuries. It was a rather straightforward claim in which he claimed he had a concussion and consequently lost business.

As I recall, he expressed plans to sue, although I'm not sure he actually filed the suit. If he did, it would have been against the *Siegfried and Roy Magic Show* and Feld Entertainment. Ultimately the issue was resolved. I recall the most fascinating portion of the experience—talking with all the folks in Las Vegas. This included the animal handlers that worked with these animals when they weren't on stage in terms of Siegfried and Roy's assistance and, in particular, Lynette Chappell, who was their longtime assistant, both on stage and off stage.

I could only talk to them about 2 a.m. East Coast time. Their day started late because the shows went late, and after the shows were over, frequently, they would eat. I never did get to meet or speak with Siegfried and Roy. With my love for magic, meeting these gentlemen would have been a highlight of my career, at least the magic portion of it. But I'm still able to say that during my career, I represented the *Greatest Show on Earth* and the *Siegfried & Roy Magic Show*. That's not something many lawyers can say.

Payne Stewart: "Do You Play Golf?"

It was a fall afternoon in 1999; I was sitting in my office in Washington when I received a phone call from an insurance company vice-president. We weren't close friends but had met, and he was aware that I did aviation legal work. I recall, in one of our previous encounters, he asked if I played golf. My typical answer when asked that question is to suggest that I don't play golf, I play at golf.

In my thinking, a round of golf is 18 separate games, and I'm fortunate enough that I don't take it so seriously that I can't enjoy it. I don't keep a record of my scores, and as I said, every hole is like a new game to me. In many respects, nine holes are perfect. On this particular day, he called and asked once again if I play golf. This short banter served as an introduction to the purpose of his call. He wanted to speak with me about the death of a professional golfer, Payne Stewart.

On a Sunday afternoon four months earlier, Stewart completed a round of golf and took his place as the winner of the *1999 U.S. Open* at Pinehurst, North Carolina. He was known not only for his impressive golf game, complete with a long, fluid motion when he swung a club but also for his throwback clothing choices. Those choices consisted of a flat cap that matched colorful knickers and coordinated knee-high socks.

Although Stewart was only 42 years old, his career on the PGA tour spanned 19 years. During that time, he won 18 tournaments. Coming into 1999, Stewart was in a slump, winning only one tournament between 1991 and 1998, but 1999 was starting to look like a banner year. In addition to the *U.S. Open*, he also finished atop the leader board at the *AT&T Pebble Beach National Pro-Am* and was on the winning U.S. *Ryder Cup* team.

Another important factor is that Stewart had experienced a significant personal transformation as well as improvement in his golf game. At the beginning of his career, many considered him to be prickly and unapproachable. That changed, and he became one of the more popular players on the Tour. Stewart understood this and even said, "The old Payne Stewart wasn't a very good guy, but this is a different Payne Stewart." Knowing all of that about the golfer makes what happened to him even more tragic.

Leaving Orlando International Airport in Florida on October 25, 1999, a Learjet 35, owned and operated by SunJet Aviation, left for Dallas Love Field. Those on board consisted of two crew members and four passengers. In command was Captain Michael Kling, a 42-year-old former Air Force pilot with more than 4,000 hours of flight time. Stephanie Bellegarrigue was the 27-year-old co-pilot, and she had more than 1,700 hours in the air. She actually had more hours in the Learjet than the Captain. The most notable passenger was golfer Payne Stewart, accompanied by his two agents and a golf course architect.

Take off time was 9:19 a.m. for the expected three-hour flight. Within minutes, the plane was under the control of

Jacksonville Air Traffic, which ordered the plane to climb to 39,000 feet. The pilots acknowledged and within minutes approached the desired altitude. The plan was to head northwest until reaching Cross City, Florida, where it would turn west, directly to Dallas. There was to be no more radio contact with the plane.

After several failed attempts at radio contact and the fact that the plane did not stop climbing when the desired altitude was reached, alerted air traffic controllers who knew that something was wrong. This fear was confirmed when the plane failed to make the planned turn to the west. An emergency was declared, and the NTSB was notified. The NTSB contacted Learjet to determine how far the plane could fly.

The media got the news, and the word was out about the out-of-control plane. Military planes were scrambled to observe and report. The fighter pilots flew close to the Learjet to see if they could determine what was going on. They reported it was difficult to see inside the plane. It appeared that ice or frost had formed on the inside of the windows, making them very opaque. Eventually, everyone was confident that neither pilot was conscious, and the plane was locked on autopilot.

The NTSB later determined the plane suffered a pressurization problem, which caused everyone on board to lose consciousness. It also suggested that everyone inside was also dead already. Once hope for the passengers and crew was lost, concern was shifted to determine where the plane might crash.

At 12:10, five hours into the flight, the plane exhausted all the fuel. At that point, it began a rapid, twisting descent, crashing into the ground in Edmunds County, South Dakota. Fortunately, the crash site was an empty field, far from buildings or people. The NTSB was never able to identify the cause of the pressurization problem conclusively. Their finding read: "Incapacitation of the flight crewmembers as a result of their failure to receive supplemental oxygen following a loss of cabin pressurization, for undetermined reasons." They were convinced the plane lost pressurization, but they found no clues as to why that happened.

There was some discussion, both during and after the event, if the fighter jets were authorized to shoot down the plane if it appeared headed toward a populated area. As I write these words, I'm not sure if that was true or not. Fortunately, the plane was headed toward a sparsely populated part of our country, and it did crash in an empty field, causing no damage on the ground.

The insurance representative who called informed me that an accident has just occurred, and they wanted to retain me as their lawyer. "We need you to go down to Orlando, Florida."

Then he quickly explained that they insured a company named Sunjet Aviation, a charter flight operation out of Sanford Airport in Orlando, which was operating the aircraft and for whom both pilots worked. One of their aircraft had crashed. He said the plane was flying north and ran out of fuel and crashed in a field.

I was accustomed to this type of call concerning an airplane crash. When he added that Payne Stewart was on board, he obviously caught my attention. I didn't know the two sports agents, but Bruce Borland, the golf course designer, worked with Jack Nicklaus' golf course design company, Golden Bear. The group was on tour to Dallas and then on to Houston, looking for property for golf course development. It would be a

Payne Stewart design golf course with the actual work done by Golden Bear.

It was a real tragedy for Sunjet. The company was located at Sanford Airport, and I wasted no time and flew down to Florida early the next morning. The media was already there and gathered outside when I arrived. I met with the owner of Sunjet. The NTSB investigation was well underway by the time I arrived.

The focus of the investigation followed the speculation from the outset that there had been a decompression. Decompression occurs when a plane is flying at an altitude where the air is unbreathable. Every jet you have flown on has been pressurized. That's why the flight attendants explain the importance of using the yellow oxygen masks that will drop down in the event of depressurization. When that Learjet lost cabin pressure, the result was that everyone inside lost consciousness.

The cause of the decompression has never been determined. Investigators were unable to establish if it was an insidious decompression, which means slow where people drift off to sleep, almost without knowing, or if it was an explosive decompression where something exploded, and the breathable air left immediately. However, it happened; it did not affect the ability of the airplane to fly. There will never be certainty as to the cause.

An interesting factor in the situation was that the Captain, an Air Force veteran, had been a high-altitude instructor and had been through the high-altitude chamber during his Air Force training. That means he had already experienced the effects of hypoxia. The purpose of that training is so the pilot will know the symptoms and be able to recognize the problem at the onset. He knew what it would do to him and the importance of responding immediately. His training was simply another clue in the investigation by the NTSB, but the devastating wreckage caused by the high-speed crash removed any clues to prove what happened.

We settled the case on behalf of Sunjet and the repair organization that was part of Sunjet. Although they were not a "common carrier" or airline in the sense that they would issue tickets, it was important to do the right thing. Given the potential for the amount of damages that could have been established because of the fame of Payne Stewart, it made a lot of sense for Sunjet and its insurers to settle with Payne Stewart's estate and those of the other two passengers.

As the days and months went by and the crash fell out of the front page news, Sunjet went about the task of rebuilding their business after all of the unflattering publicity. Any fatal airline accident results in the operator enduing a great deal of scrutiny. That's a lot of our work—helping them after the investigation to manage and stay on top of FAA related issues. We also provide guidance concerning the media, what to expect, and what they can and cannot say.

The accident occurred in October 1999. In April of 2000, the premises of Sunjet Aviation were raided by the FBI and local police at the behest of a grand jury. They gathered up operating records and logs of all the aircraft on-site, seizing computers and other items. As you can imagine, employees felt frightened and intimidated, and the business was shut down. Once again, the news media made Sunjet infamous.

The owner of Sunjet called to tell me that the FBI showed up at their facility with subpoenas just as their charter business had returned. It didn't make any sense to him since there was no fault attributed to the company, and there were no accusations that the pilots performed inappropriately.

I told him what I tell every client is that one of the things that occur following an aviation accident is a district attorney or some U.S. attorney looking for their 15 minutes of fame. They convene a grand jury, and next have the FBI conduct a raid with a search warrant. People are hustled out of the building, and all the documents are boxed up and hauled off, and it looks great on the evening news.

The company owner was standing outside his building when he called me and described the FBI agents in their windbreakers as they loaded up his files. I had to tell him there's nothing much to do. The tragedy of the story is the Sunjet was getting its business back and continuing to move forward. Nobody had been in a position to attribute fault or blame for failures or sloppy operation or anything. Yet, what happened is because of all the renewed publicity and the FBI turning it into a media event and the U.S. attorney's office involving a grand jury, the company ended up in bankruptcy. There was never an indictment that led to criminal proceedings, and the whole thing went nowhere.

I tell every client that we have, especially airlines and charter operators, that when an accident occurs, three are a multitude of trains that leave the station, and they wait for no person. One of them is the NTSB investigation. Others include civil litigation, the 24/7 news cycle, employees and how to deal with them, and former disgruntled employees. Sometimes, employees don't even know they're disgruntled until there's a criminal investigation.

Unlike many foreign countries, we don't criminalize aviation accidents in this country, thankfully. To criminalize means to charge pilots and companies with criminal conduct for accidents. At that point, they would, if we did criminalize accidents in the U.S., invoke their Fifth Amendment rights, and the NTSB will never be able to investigate accidents, and aviation will not maintain the current levels of safety. Investigations are accurate and effective because participants are allowed to talk without fear of being charged with a crime.

However, I always assume there's an investigation by some district attorney or similar prosecutor. Virtually, one hundred percent of the time, they go nowhere because the conduct doesn't rise to the level of criminal conduct.

There is one exception when there was actually a criminal prosecution that involved ValuJet and an accident in Florida in 1995. In that case, a company packaged and labeled expired chemical oxygen generators and returned them to ValuJet for shipment and further repair. The NTSB concluded that shortly after takeoff, the canisters ignited and caused the crash. The defendants were convicted at trial on felony murder and manslaughter charges, but the charges were vacated on appeal. The appeals court stated that the repair people made mistakes, but they did not commit a crime; there was no intention to kill the victims of the accident.

In this country, we don't put flight crews in jail, and we don't lock up air traffic controllers. That doesn't mean the FBI won't show up at your office and make life difficult. As Sunjet experienced, it might even drive you into bankruptcy.

The loss of human life is always a tragedy, and it's compounded when the victim is a celebrity or a great champion. But, another victim of that accident was Sunjet. They were recovering well from the initial tragedy, yet found themselves, by virtue of somebody's agenda, on the receiving end of an FBI search warrant, putting them on the evening news and the morning newspaper. The fact that the entire case was ultimately dropped did nothing to help Sunjet stay in business.

F. Lee Bailey

Handling aviation legal cases involving the government means that interesting stuff will cross your desk at times. The most memorable are usually the most tragic, especially when it involves a major airline crash. However, one memorable lawsuit assigned to me while at the Justice Department involved Enstrom Helicopter.

Enstrom had filed a lawsuit against the United States, specifically the Federal Aviation Administration. Since it is not legal to sue the FAA by name, you have to sue the United States, which is how I got involved through the DOJ. The suit revolved around the theory of negligent certification of the helicopter fuel system by the FAA.

Enstrom Helicopter began designing and building helicopters in Michigan in 1957. The pilot in the case of this particular lawsuit was David Bailey (not related to F. Lee Bailey), and he had one passenger on board. It was a demonstration flight, so the passenger, a reporter, could write a review of the Enstrom Interceptor helicopter. The aircraft was a short distance off the coast near Santa Monica, California, actually within sight of the beach. It was one of those days when the weather is great for

123

a trip to the beach, so there were numerous people along the shore.

At some point in the flight, the fuel system stopped feeding fuel to the engine. Like any motor with no fuel, it shut down. The helicopter lost power and crashed into the water. Fortunately, neither the pilot nor the passenger was killed, only minor injuries. However, the helicopter was destroyed. Folks on the beach who had been waiting for the surf ran into the water to help the two men who were in the helicopter.

The investigation showed that the aircraft had plenty of fuel, but for reasons that were not clear, the fuel was not making it to the engine. It would be like driving a car with a full tank of gas, but for some reason, the fuel doesn't get pumped to the engine. That's not such a big deal in a car since you can coast to the side of the road. In a helicopter, or plane, it's a different story; you're going to go down. Thankfully in this incident, no one was seriously injured.

The lawsuit was filed alleging that the FAA, which had certified the helicopter, had been negligent in certifying the craft and particularly the fuel system. Since the lawsuit was directed toward the FAA, the case was handled by the Department of Justice. As the trial lawyer for the Aviation Unit, I received a copy of the complaint that had been filed in court. I also gathered other necessary documents about the accident and the company.

Early in the process, my research revealed that F. Lee Bailey was the owner of Enstrom Helicopter. Of course, F. Lee Bailey was a famous trial lawyer. By that time, he had already successfully defended Dr. Sam Sheppard on his retrial for murder charges, and it was before the Patty Hearst case in San

Francisco. He was a regular guest on the *Tonight Show* and had written several best-selling books. His background included being a Marine pilot, so he had an overriding interest in aviation. In addition to owning the helicopter factory, Bailey had his own Lear Jet.

I took the pilot's deposition and read the investigative documents along with the handbook for the aircraft, and it became apparent there was nothing wrong with the fuel system. The FAA hadn't done anything wrong. Years later, the Supreme Court, in an unrelated case, ruled that it was not legal to sue the United States for negligent certification of an airplane.

I also concluded that Mr. Bailey, the pilot, was flying the helicopter incorrectly. In his witness statement, he described a specific maneuver that was contrary to the operating handbook for the aircraft. As I recall, there was a warning in the handbook that such a maneuver could cut off fuel to the engine. In helicopter pilot jargon, it was the difference between a slip and a slide-type maneuver. In his deposition, the pilot indicated he had performed in a way that the handbook warns against.

To be thorough meant I also need to depose the owner of the company. Taking a deposition from F. Lee Bailey was a memorable experience. As I was growing up, I always watched the *Perry Mason* television show featuring Raymond Burr. Each show lasted only one hour, commercials included. During those 60 minutes, amazing things happened. An accused criminal retained *Perry Mason*; the entire trial would happen, and usually, during the trial, the real murderer was exposed. *Perry Mason*, a character created by Earl Stanley Gardner, served as a role model for me, and I longed for some of those *Perry Mason* moments.

At this stage of his career, F. Lee Bailey was something of a living *Perry Mason*. When it came to his deposition, the first thing that happened was a motion to quash to prevent me from even taking his deposition. It was filed by a lawyer from his office in Boston. The basic thrust was that F. Lee Bailey is too busy to give a deposition. We wrote a response and explained that if he's not too busy to file a lawsuit, but too busy to give a deposition, we'll accommodate his schedule in any way. The court overruled the motion to quash and ordered that he appear for a deposition. I did, in fact, accommodate his schedule, and we met in the office of the lawyer representing Enstrom on a day that worked for F. Lee Bailey.

To this day, I remember taking the Washington Metro subway from my office at the DOJ to the lawyer's office. Standing on the platform waiting for the train, I had a difficult time trying to fathom what I was doing. I couldn't believe that I was going to take F. Lee Bailey's deposition. Arriving at the office, I was directed to the conference room. When he entered the room, he looked just like he appeared on television. I introduced myself, and he was sworn in as a witness by the court reporter. When I asked his name, I think he said, "Francis Lee Bailey," I'm not totally sure. It was a potent experience.

I followed up by asking for his address, and he provided the office address in Boston. Then I asked for his occupation. I remember his answer to this day. He said he was an "attorney, author, lecturer, and manufacturer." Those four occupations summed up his life at that stage. As the deposition continued, he endorsed or confirmed my theory as to what caused the accident. It was a productive session, and ultimately the case went away. I honestly don't recall how. I think it might have been dismissed based on the testimony of Mr. Bailey, the pilot, and F. Lee Bailey, the owner. The fact that this was a pilot error meant it had nothing to do with what the FAA had done or not done.

A number of years later, when I was defending the United States in the Korean Airlines 007 litigation involving the Soviet shootdown of a 747 aircraft, Lee Bailey showed up again. This time he was one of the plaintiff's lawyers but not heavily involved in the case. He was at one of the depositions of Korean Airlines pilots who provided testimony about the airlines and flying procedures. Both pilots in the crash were killed and obviously not a part of the trial.

I'm convinced that every one of the Korean Airline pilots spoke English because it's the global language for aviation. However, the lawyers for Korean Airlines refused to allow them to testify in English. We had to use translators, but even then, F. Lee Bailey confirmed what I wanted to believe about him in terms of being a good lawyer. He took the best deposition of any of the plaintiff's lawyers in that case. It was concise, direct, and targeted. He didn't waste a lot of time asking about peripheral issues. He pinned down the pilot to the relevant matters and did a heck of a good job.

I ran into him again on an airplane after that case was complete. I was flying to Las Vegas, where I had been invited to speak on a panel. As I boarded the airplane, walking through first class on my way back to my seat, I saw Bailey sitting in first class. I stopped for a second, and he recognized me. He asked why I was going to Las Vegas. I told him about the conference, although I knew he was on one of the panels as well as the featured speaker for the whole event. Before I stepped away, he told me that he would wait for me once we got off the plane, and I could ride with him to the hotel. I thought it was very gracious, and sure enough, he was there with his wife or girlfriend waiting for me, and we walked to the baggage claim together. He was met by what was essentially an entourage, including a driver. We climbed into a big limousine from the hotel for the ride.

When we arrived at the hotel, I checked into my room. It was already quite late, so I went to bed and was asleep when I heard pounding on my door. It was probably about one in the morning. Since my day started in the Eastern Time Zone, it was late. I got up and answered the door. It was Lee Bailey, and he just walked in. Somehow he got my room number from the hotel. He sat down, and we spent the next two or three hours talking. It was a once-in-a-lifetime opportunity—spending two hours listening to F. Lee Bailey, one of the most prominent trial lawyers in America. As suddenly as he came in, he got up, said good night, and left.

The next day, I saw him for a short two minutes before he spoke. My panel was finished, and I was getting ready to head back to the airport. I honestly think he was a superb trial lawyer, notwithstanding any other issues he may have encountered later in his career. What strikes me is that he was so busy any time I talked with him, I felt he was already, at least in his mind, at the next conversation with somebody else, somewhere else. He was operating ahead of real-time.

Many years later, I wrote a book called *Dombroff on Unfair Tactics*. I was very gratified that F. Lee Bailey was willing to write the forward to the first edition. He was complimentary in writing that the book will be a standard text in a profession which badly needs "more simulators" of Mr. Dombroff's effort. The following is F. Lee Bailey's Foreword to my book:

Ever since I tried my first lawsuit 30 years ago at the tender age of 21, I have been a consistent critic of the meager legal training afforded our prospective trial lawyers. The efforts of various law schools vary widely in attacking this problem, but none has succeeded, in my opinion, in a meaningful way.

The handling of a lawsuit demands considerable talent from those in charge. They are warriors, compromisors, conciliators, and mediators, possessing, hopefully, a combination of fearlessness and good judgment. Entrusted to them are enormous stakes, ranging from huge sums of money to human life itself. In an adversarial system of regulating disputes in human affairs, trial lawyers are critically important to society, for the published results of their advocacy exert a pervasive influence on the judgment of the many who do not go to the mat, but are interested in telling their clients where the point of wise compromise may lie.

As in every undertaking, there is a limit to what can be taught short of actual field experience. In the case of early airmen, the perimeters of safe flight had to be learned by each pilot in an airplane with a crash the price of a mistake. As aviation has progressed, we have used simulators to "teach out" those mistakes most frequently made without paying twisted aluminum and injury or death as the price of a slip.

In legal practice, as Chief Justice Burger has been saying for some years now, we need better training of this type. A trained person is by definition one who avoids those mistakes which an untrained person does not perceive, or perceives too late to make timely corrections. And while we use simulators of a sort in legal training, called "moot courts," the bulk of what lawyers learn about mistake avoidance is done at the expense of real clients in real cases. This unfortunate circumstance is tantamount to training young surgeons on actual triple by-pass cases, or student pilots in the cockpits of commercial airliners. The pressure is and should remain upon the profession to make greater use of simulators and less use of live clients in the training process.

This book is an answer to that challenge. An office lawyer is a force who does work with whatever time may be required to reflect and revise, to consult with colleagues, and to redraft as often as the need for a good product may require. A trial lawyer is a power force with a time factor who often gets only one chance to make a quick decision on a particular issue, and thus has a much greater chance of making a mistake. The avoidance of mistakes in a fast-changing environment requires the ability to anticipate what is next to come, judge the availability of numerous options, and rapidly select the best option available. No lawyer can ever confront every possible dilemma in trial practice under circumstances where he or she can calmly sort out the options and carefully reason the way to the best decision. To accomplish this end, the advocate must draw on personal experience and the experiences of others. This book is chock-full of such experience, setting forth the options commonly available, and the pros and cons which flow from the selection of each option.

Strategy is an armchair or a conference game, where long-range plans are worked out, organized, and committed to the war. Tactics involve the skirmishes of battle under ever-changing conditions, where experience and knowledge must be swiftly applied to the circumstances at hand. This book is about that more difficult area—tactics. While the partners in the boardroom may map out the strategy, the advocate on the front lines is responsible for tactical decisions. This book is in my judgment of immense value to trial lawyers at all levels, from those new at the game to seasoned professionals. It offers a wealth of pointers on mistake avoidance by example after example, by discussing the options likely to accompany each decision-confrontation and by giving the advice of an experienced field general as to how those options should be evaluated. I have tried many cases of many sorts in many jurisdictions, and yet I found myself constantly learning new twists and nuances as I read through this book.

I strongly recommend it to my colleagues at the Bar. For lawyers over whom l have the power of direction in my own practice, it will be required reading. And if I succeed in helping to establish-as I have promised for many years to do-a specialized course for the training of advocates leading to a Master's Degree in Advocacy, this book will be a standard text. In a profession which badly needs more simulators, I view Mr. Dombroff's effort as a quantum leap forward.

Perry Mason Moment: Pago Pago

I grew up watching *Perry Mason*, starring Raymond Burr. The cast of characters included Paul Drake, the private investigator, and Della Street, Mason's trusted assistant. It was a big show when it was on, and given the fact that both my parents were lawyers, I always assumed I would be a lawyer growing up. Even today, I watch reruns and have read the Stanley Gardner books the show was based on. It's amazing that in one hour of television (less if you account for commercials), Mason would investigate, craft a defense, and unveil the real murderer in a courtroom climax.

That courtroom climax is what I call a *Perry Mason* Moment. It's a time when the audience senses an *aha* as Perry revealed the murderer and proved his client's innocence. I think every lawyer looks for that *Perry Mason* Moment in their career. Court cases indeed take much more than an hour, sometimes years, and more often than not, they are straightforward without any fireworks. The *Perry Mason* Moment rarely presents itself during a lawyer's career.

In 1974, when I was at the Department of Justice as a trial attorney, a Pan American Airways Boeing 707 crashed at the airport at Pago Pago. The flight had 101 passengers and crew members on board, and 97 died, leaving only four survivors. The crash occurred at night as the plane approached the runway, but fell short. When it hit the ground, it skidded until striking a volcanic dike that ran perpendicular to the runway. It seems that everyone survived the impact, but the deaths were the result of smoke inhalation from the fire.

Lawsuits were filed or consolidated in Los Angeles by families of the survivors as well as the four survivors. The plaintiff sued Pan American World Airways, Boeing, the manufacturer of the airplane, and the Federal Aviation Administration of the United States. I was assigned to defend the United States. The allegation against Pan Am was that they were negligent in the way they operated the flight. It focused not only on what happened on that day, January 30, 1974, but also on the broader subjects of training and standards.

Allegations against Boeing had to do with crashworthiness and flammability of the interior of the aircraft since smoke inhalation from the fire was the cause of death. The cause of action against the US, among other things, asserted that navigational aids were faulty. The navigation system at the airport had been installed and maintained by the United States

The judge who was assigned the case began hearing motions, but it was transferred to Judge William Matthew Byrne, Jr. He was relatively new on the bench, having served previously as the US Attorney for Central California. His biggest claim to fame as a judge was that he was involved with the case of the Pentagon Papers.

A substantial amount of discovery was taken. In fact, at times, the discovery process, especially the depositions of sworn testimony outside of court, became so contentious among lawyers that the judge before Judge Byrne, Judge Pierson Hall, had appointed a special master. Aubrey Irwin was a retired state court judge who presided as a judge over depositions, and he ordered the depositions to take place in the Federal Courthouse.

For months on end, for over a year and a half, I commuted to Los Angeles, taking depositions in an unused Magistrate's courtroom. The room was smaller than a Federal Judge's court. The Special Master sat at the Magistrate's bench, and the witness who was being deposed sat in a witness chair along with a court reporter and lawyers in the room. It was like sitting in a mini-court. In a normal deposition, there is no judge or special master. Lawyers can make objections, and those objections ultimately get resolved by the trial judge, but in this case, the Special Master ruled immediately. If the plaintiffs asked for a document from the United States, and we objected for some reason, or we felt the request was too broad and didn't have time limits, we filed our objections, and the Special Master ruled on them. He was basically acting as a judge. We could appeal to the Federal Judge, but that was rare, and I'm not sure Judge Byrne would have overruled the Special Master. One of the reasons the predecessor Federal Judge had appointed the Special Master was so he didn't have to deal with the case, which had become very acrimonious, on a day-by-day basis.

The Special Master was Judge Aubrey Irwin. He was a nice enough fellow, and I'm not sure he made a lot of bad rulings, but it did slow down the process in many respects. The parties didn't move as quickly through the depositions, as was typical.

As the case was being prepared for trial, the plaintiffs needed to get past what's called the Warsaw Limits. The Warsaw Convention is an international agreement which limited the amount of money plaintiffs could get from Pan Am unless they could prove willful misconduct. It's more than negligence. It's a knowing violation of the law or a reasonable standard of care, typically for economic gain. The plaintiff's theory was that Pan Am was carrying extra fuel onboard that particular Boeing 707. Fuel was much cheaper in New Zealand, so according to plaintiffs, they carried more than called for due to economic reasons, thereby changing some of the operating characteristics of the airplane due to increased weight.

An important aspect of the case against the United States revolved around the glide slope. It's a part of the Instrument Landing System (ILS) that allows pilots to land in conditions of limited visibility. Think of it as an electronic exit ramp that takes an airplane down to the runway. The electronic glide slope is an angled highway in the sky, pointing from the runway up to a point in the sky that the airplane intercepts it. The system at Pago Pago was steeper than normal because of the mountainous terrain at the end of the runway. The FAA establishes clearance limits and formulas. It was well-known that this particular glide slope was steeper than normal, and it was published on all the approach charts used by pilots. When the glide slope is steeper, the rate of descent is higher to the end of the runway. This means a shorter time to get down and land on the runway.

In the case of the Pago Pago flight, it was an airplane with a higher rate of descent coupled with a heavier than normal plane because of the extra fuel. The plaintiffs asserted willful misconduct as to carrying the extra fuel, and that it should result in the removal of the per-passenger monetary cap on recoveries.

The trial consisted essentially of the plaintiffs versus Pan Am and Boeing, and then Pan Am pointing the finger at the United States. If I had been a plaintiff's lawyer, I would have done the same thing. My approach would have been to rely on Pan Am to establish my case as a plaintiff against the United States, so, as a plaintiff, I could focus on pointing the finger at Pan Am and Boeing.

It was a long trial. It took months to unfold, and I was commuting from Washington, where I lived. The accident was in 1974, and the trial started in 1978, almost four years later. That's not unusual because accident investigations can take a year or two before a final report is issued. Litigation typically doesn't really begin until that report is issued. It makes sense to let the government do all the investigating and use it as a starting point for discovery in the litigation.

The trial finally started in January 1978, and all I did was commute. I was married in 1973, so I would either fly out on Sunday night or Monday morning. Court would typically start on Monday afternoon, and then I took the red-eye on Friday night to get back home. The trial absolutely consumed me. This was before computers to manage documents. I had devised an elaborate trial organization system that worked extraordinarily well. I called it *Litidex* and wrote some articles about it.

I worked out of an office that had been used by the US Marshals office in Los Angeles. We were in a big empty room that had a holding cell on one side of the room. We set up in the holding cell and sometimes felt as if we were prisoners in Los Angeles. It seemed appropriate.

Over the course of the months of trial, I worked out of this jail cell turned office, and I had one new lawyer assisting me who had joined the DOJ just before the trial started. He was a terrific guy, formerly an Assistant United States Attorney in San Diego. He knew nothing about aviation, which meant he knew nothing about the case. He was there to assist me to the extent he could. Although he was a good guy, it boiled down to just me, not even any paralegals. When I needed something, I talked to the Civil Division of the US Attorney's office for help, and this was long before cell phones. I was basically a one-man show. It was a big case to which I had devoted a number of years and was personally invested.

After trial every day, I returned to the Ambassador Hotel, long gone, in Los Angeles. I had the daily transcript that I would read and mark up with notes while having dinner. After that bed. I never went out or anywhere except the hotel and court-house. But it was an extraordinary experience from a young tri-al lawyer's perspective. At the time the trial started, I had been practicing law for eight years, and I had no idea as to the num-ber of issues and situations that would present themselves, and one of them was a *Perry Mason* Moment.

The principal argument by Pan Am against the United States at trial had to do with a concept introduced by their ex-perts called *reverse sensing*. The argument was that when a pilot uses the electronic glide slope, an electronic beam leads him to the runway. A signal received in the cockpit instructs whether he should fly up or down. If above the signal, then fly down; if below the signal, then fly up. It's necessary to stay on the sig-nal. Keeping the instrument centered will lead directly to the runway.

Pan Am argued that the runway at Pago Pago suffered what they called *reverse sensing*. Instead of seeing directions to "fly up" if the airplane was below the glide slope, the pilot saw a "fly down," and vice versa. They claimed that the pilot was given completely misleading information, which resulted in flying into the ground short of the runway.

Had that theory of *reverse sensing* been true, there would have been some substance to the argument since the plane landed with some visibility limitations during rain showers and might have focused strictly on the glide slope. They couldn't see the ground and had no independent means of verifying whether they were in the appropriate position. Of course, other issues were involved, but that was the thrust of Pan Am's argument.

During the pre-trial preparation phases of the case, I had been identifying and looking for experts. I went to the FAA for an expert because the glide slope at Pago Pago had been installed and maintained by the FAA. It was their navigation system, and if there was something wrong with the navigation system and it sends out a wrong signal, that would be negligence, and the government would have liability. The FAA put me in contact with a fellow named Dr. Richard McFarland.

I have this mental picture of the first time I met Dr. McFarland. He was exactly what I would have expected. He was an electronics engineer at Ohio University in Athens, Ohio. He was a consultant to the FAA, and the university had contracts with the FAA regarding the glide slope navigation systems, and it was apparent that Dr. MacFarland was unquestionably the world's foremost authority on this stuff.

I'm a great believer in making sure experts are fully prepared. In addition to reviewing the documents regarding the history of the glide slope, I arranged for Richard to fly to Pago Pago, American Samoa, on an FAA flight test aircraft and physically inspect the glide slope. On the flight, the inspection aircraft did inflight testing of the glideslope. They tested its angle and strength. They tested everything associated with the glide slope. He inspected the terrain, the clearances, the installation, and the equipment. He reviewed the logs. He did everything firsthand, and his opinion was that there was nothing wrong with the glide slope. There was certainly no such *reverse sensing* in American Samoa the night of the crash.

Pan American also had an expert who had been at the FAA and had worked in the glide slope area. He was Matthew Frampton from the Los Angeles area. He testified on behalf of Pan Am regarding *reverse sensing*. He went to great lengths regarding it and put up in front of the jury copies of the flight check recordings that showed the flight checks from before the accident, probably for a year or so of the Pago Pago glide slope records. If you think about an EKG, that's essentially what the flight check recorder produces. Its an EKG of the ILS system, the electronic highway to the runway.

If you have the maintenance logs that record all of the checks of the equipment on the ground and so forth and you have the flight check recordings, which the FAA retains, you get a history of the glide slope. He took great pains to demonstrate his point. I remember he was standing next to the recordings, the original recordings. They were on an easel, and he was pointing out all of the examples of *reverse sensing*, and I remember my initial sense of panic and getting up and walking across the courtroom, which was always filled with people. I walked over to see what he was talking about because, honestly, that was the first time I had ever heard of reverse sensing.

It was not something that he had testified to during any deposition or discovery. Now, at trial, in front of the jury, he disclosed the fact that the system was operating improperly and caused the airplane to fly into the ground. I'll confess being somewhat alarmed because it undercut the entire premise of Richard McFarland's opinions and testimony. I remember walking slowly, trying to contain my impatience back to my table and sitting down. Richard was sitting at the counsel table with me so that I could confer with him. I sat down and leaned over as Frampton continued to testify and whispered in his ear something to the effect of "what in the hell is going on, what does he mean reverse sensing," and Richard didn't respond.

Dr. McFarland was what you would expect as an academic at that level. He had a slide rule, or maybe even a calculator that he wore on his belt. He was a very academic looking guy, but incredibly bright and able to express himself. Without responding to me, he stood up and walked over and looked at what Frampton was pointing at to illustrate these repeated examples of *reverse sensing* on the flight check recordings. According to Pan Am's theory, the pilot received misleading information causing the accident. It would be like the navigation system in your car, instead of telling you to turn left, told you to go right, and if you had no choice but to rely on the system, you might drive into a lake or something.

Richard examined the diagram for about a minute. Then he came back slowly to our table and sat down. I immediately leaned over to him, and he whispered in my ear. I'll never forget these words, "He's reading it backward."

I was stunned. I was absolutely stunned. I don't think I realized at that moment that my *Perry Mason* Moment had come, but the idea that I was sitting in a federal courtroom defending the United States, and an expert for an area involving glide slopes, which was at the core of their case against us, was reading the chart backward was beyond my comprehension.

I sat there, listening to the direct testimony. Ultimately it ended, and I had the opportunity to cross-examine. It was late, so we adjourned for the day.

I talked to Richard and asked, "What do you mean he's reading it backward?"

He described that because of the physical location of American Samoa in the middle of the Pacific between Hawaii and Auckland, New Zealand, the FAA had a memorandum of understanding and agreement with the New Zealand flight check authorities. Fifty percent of the flight checks in American Samoa were done by the FAA and the other half by New Zealand authorities. Richard explained that the New Zealand flight check authorities reverse the polarity of their recorders, so they are directly opposite the polarity of the recorders on the FAA flight check aircraft. It's like reading from right to left when they should be read left to right, or top to bottom instead of bottom to top. For the recordings in the United States, the top is up, but with the New Zealand flight check recordings, the bottom is up.

Frampton was assuming that you read the New Zealand flight check documents the same way you read the FAA flight check documents. Richard took our copies of the recordings and walked me through them. There were annotations on those recordings that had been entered by the flight check inspector who was watching the recording being made. It's like a doctor writing notes on the EKG recording as it comes out of the recorder when you're hooked up.

When you matched the top of New Zealand recordings with the bottom of the FAA recordings, it became apparent there was no *reverse sensing*. He was reading it backward. I was having a difficult time processing this information because things like that don't happen in a trial. The idea of such a fundamental error in expert testimony that is a central part of the case was surprising, no, shocking!! It meant the case was going to come crashing down around a *Perry Mason* Moment if properly handled.

I wanted Richard to confirm what we already knew. I absolutely trusted Richard but wanted him bulletproof for our direct examination later. I asked him, during the overnight recess, to call the folks at the New Zealand flight check authorities in Auckland and to confirm it, and that's exactly what he did. He knew the head of flight check at the New Zealand authorities because he had consulted for them in the past. He got the guy out of bed and described what was going on. He confirmed overnight, before my cross-examination of Mr. Frampton had started, the fact that indeed they reverse the polarity, and you read their recordings opposite the way you read the FAA flight check recordings.

The next day it was my turn. I had a difficult time containing myself because I knew what I had. I began by going through several preliminaries. I established the fact that he had never traveled to American Samoa. He had never examined the actual ILS system. He had never been on a flight check. He had never seen the equipment, all of which Richard McFarland had done.

I asked Mr. Frampton whether or not he'd ever had any interactions with the New Zealand flight check authorities and established that he had not. I took him back over and had him repeat the answers he gave in direct examination. It wasn't word-for-word, but it was probably not far from word-for-word of his testimony on direct examination, especially with respect to *reverse sensing*, which he said was dangerous and caused the airplane to crash. I had him get up and go through all the re-cordings again and demonstrate the *reverse sensing* to the jury. I re-emphasized this extraordinarily damaging testimony to the government I was defending.

In rehashing his testimony, at least on the surface, I proba-bly broke every cardinal rule of cross-examination. Normally, I don't cross-examine a witness unless there is one of two things you can accomplish. One is if you can impeach them, and the other is if you can get helpful testimony that hasn't been testi-fied to on direct. On this occasion, none of the testimony I was getting was new, except that he had not done the work I asked him about. I was not impeaching him. I was simply re-empha-sizing this damaging testimony.

It was clear in looking at Judge Byrne on the bench, and I could almost see the quizzical look on his face, he was thinking, "Do you know what you're doing, Sir? You're simply hurting your own case."

I think there came the point that Judge Byrne knew there was a rabbit in the hat, and I was getting ready to pull it out.

Ironically, on that day, the Chief Justice of the Israeli Supreme Court was a guest of the court and was actually on the bench with Judge Byrne. The judge introduced him that morning. Even though he was an observer, there was a lot of whispering as the day proceeded between Judge Byrne and the Chief Justice of the Israeli Supreme Court.

I was setting up Frampton, and then the *Perry Mason* Moment came when I asked, "Isn't it true, sir, that you are simply reading the New Zealand flight check recordings, which you have testified in great detail demonstrate this dangerous condition of reverse sensing, isn't it true that you are reading them backward?"

There was an eruption in the courtroom. The Pan Am lawyer jumped up and started objecting and shouting that there's no foundation for this. I just stood there and let the noise wash over me. The judge banged his gavel and told him to sit down and said, "Mr. Dombroff, you may proceed."

I continued, "Sir, you're reading these recordings backward."

Frampton responded, "No, it's not possible."

I said, "Sir, you're reading these recording backward because the polarities of the recorder are reversed on the New Zealand flight check authorities. Down is, in fact, down, and up is, in fact, up, whether you're looking at the New Zealand recordings or the FAA recordings so long as you understand that the recordings are different because of the reverse polarity."

Mr. Frampton continued to claim that what I was saying was not possible. At that point, I took him through the annotations and said, "Sir, that annotation on the New Zealand flight check recording makes no sense whatsoever if there's reverse sensing as shown by this recording as you have testified."

He couldn't answer, and then I took him to the next annotation and the next. He continued to deny everything and said it wasn't possible, and they didn't reverse the polarity, and it wasn't possible. Everybody in that courtroom knew that he was just a hundred percent wrong that he had read the recordings backward. It was a moment that I had never had before, and I suspect most lawyers will never have. I was very fortunate.

I also used my cross-examination of Mr. Frampton to prepare for my expert, Richard McFarland. I had Mr. Frampton acknowledge that Richard was one of the world's foremost authorities on glide slope systems. Feeling that wasn't good enough, I said, "Sir, he is **the** leading world authority on the glide slope system, isn't he?"

When it was time for Richard to testify, I began by establishing his credentials and the fact that he had gone to American Samoa on the flight check aircraft and actually inspected the system, and that he spoke to New Zealand flight check authorities. My questioning went like this:

"Were you here during the testimony of Mr. Frampton?" I asked.

He responded affirmatively, and I continued, "Was Mr. Frampton reading the flight check, the New Zealand flight check recordings correctly?"

He replied, "No, he was not. He was reading them backward."

Moving on, I said, "Is there any evidence of reverse sensing in any document that has seen in this entire matter?"

"None, whatsoever."

Richard blew them out of the water. It was truly a *Perry Mason* moment.

In his well-researched book about the crash in Pago Pago, William Norris wrote these words: "…it seems probable that Frampton knew (nothing) of the two great passions of Mark

Dombroff's private life: his work as a semiprofessional magician, under the pseudonym of 'Mark Andrew,' and his obsession with the cases of *Perry Mason*. The combination was formidable. Dombroff was a man who delighted in pulling rabbits out of hats, and he had an insatiable taste for courtroom drama. When he stepped up to do battle with Frampton, he was employing both talents fully. (William Norris, "Willful Misconduct: The Shocking Story of Pan American Flight 806 and its Startling Aftermath" p152.)

This trial was early in my career, and it was not my last big moment in the courtroom. In fact, it was not even the only big moment I had in this trial. Another *Perry Mason* Moment occurred with another Pan Am expert, David Hodges. We'll meet him in the next chapter.

Pago Pago: "If a Tree Falls in the Forest..."

Since you're not entitled to a jury when you sue the United States, the Pan Am Flight 806 crash in Pago Pago was the first jury trial of my career. It provided several other firsts as we moved our way toward a verdict. One of them involved an expert witness named David Alexander Hodges. He testified on behalf of Pan Am as they attempted to prove that a power failure was another culprit causing the plane to touchdown short of the runway.

In addition to *reverse sensing,* another theory they posited was that a power outage occurred as the airplane was on approach and all the runway lights went out. This would have greatly contributed to the pilots missing the end of the runway. It had already been established that rainstorms and wind occurred that night, so it was a natural leap for Pan Am to develop a theory that placed some of the blame for the crash on the weather.

The fact is that the cause of the accident was pilot error. The pilots did not comply with the checklists. They did not make call-outs. They completely screwed up the approach to the runway. Pan Am's defense rested on the theories of *reverse sensing* presented by Mr. Frampton and a power outage presented by Mr. Hodges.

The power outage theory claimed that a palm tree fell on power lines during the storm. Mr. Hodges brought a fully functioning model to demonstrate his theory. I remember sitting there as he testified about the palm tree, and on his model, he had a little model of a palm tree resting on a hinge. There were little wires, representing the above-ground power lines, wired up to carry a current from a battery to a light bulb at the other end of the display. As he testified, he knocked over the palm tree, and it shorted out the wires, and the light bulb went out. He used it to demonstrate how a fallen palm knocked out the power to the runway.

By the way, this case provided the first major use of demonstrative evidence in my career. I had a large model, not only of the Pago Pago airport but also the entire approach path. It was about the size of a shuffleboard table, and it was built to scale. Model makers in the FBI laboratory made the model. Their job was to create models for large criminal cases, including the assassinations of Dr. King and John Kennedy. My model far surpassed the level of sophistication of the one made by Mr. Hodges, but he was undaunted as he showed his model to the jury to demonstrate his theory of a power outage.

As Mr. Hodges explained his theory, I remember sitting there searching my mind for any evidence that had been developed, or any record, document, or testimony that indicated a power outage at the airport. There was, in fact, evidence of a *blackout* from the operator of the Combined Approach Pacific International Station (CAPIS), the hybrid facility of the FAA at Pago Pago, since there was not an air traffic control tower.

Frank Bateman was the operator at CAPIS and was talking with the airplanes, not to give clearances as an air traffic controller, but rather to pass general information. He revealed there was a rainstorm between him and the airplane, and he couldn't see the lights on the plane. There was also communication from the airplane, indicating they couldn't see the lights at the runway. Heavy rain between Mr. Bateman and the airplane explained lights being obscured, and there was absolutely no evidence of a power failure. There were no records of anyone from the utility provider or the airport or any reports regarding a power failure.

Mr. Hodges also suggested that if there were power outages or fluctuations, the glide slope would essentially power down. The analogy is a light bulb in a room with a dimmer switch. When you turn the power down on the dimmer switch, the light bulb gets dimmer and then brighter when the power is increased. When I spoke on the phone with Mr. McFarland and asked him about that possibility, he described how it was not possible. The power supply to the ILS didn't operate on the level of power. It was on and stayed on until the power was nearly completely cut off. It was not like the brightness of a bulb. Reducing power made no difference.

When I got up to cross-examine Mr. Hodges and his palm tree theory, it was another *Perry Mason* Moment. I asked him to explain his palm tree theory once again. As he answered, I knocked his palm tree over into the wires with my finger.

Then I said, "By the way, Sir, did you see a single piece of evidence anywhere, a record, testimony, anything which indicated that there was ever a power failure caused by a palm tree striking wires?"

He responded, "No."

"Did you see any record of a repairman going out?" I continued.

"No."

"Did you see any evidence that the lighting system had to be reset?"

Again, he said, "No."

What's noteworthy is that if the runway lights and approach lights went out, they had to be manually reset. It required that someone go to an electrical box and reset the lights. There was no evidence they had ever been reset, much less the lights ever went out.

My questions continued, "Did you ever go to Pago Pago?"

"No."

"Did you ever see any pictures of palm trees lying across power lines?"

"No."

Then I said, "Sir, really all you've done is make this all up. Isn't that right?"

Pan Am lawyers immediately objected as you might expect, and I said, "I'll withdraw the question, your Honor, no further questions."

It was pretty extraordinary.

As to his so-called "power fluctuations," the demonstration constructed by Mr. Hodges allowed him to reduce power to an electric motor to demonstrate that by reducing the power, a motor he wired in with the lights operated at slower speeds and dimmed the lights. However, that's not the way the system at Pago Pago worked, as I explained earlier.

One of the great things about representing the United States is that awesome resources are available. I had Richard McFarland locate an airport with the same ILS system as Pago Pago. There was one at Miami International Airport. Working with the FAA, we took the black box component that was an absolutely identical copy as Pago Pago and flew it from Miami to Los Angeles over the weekend.

I took it with me to court on Monday, and using the two wires Mr. Hodges had hooked up to his model, which was not in any way similar to Pago Pago's system, I was able to get electricity. We turned it on, and it operated at 1800 RPM. Then I had Mr. Hodges turn the power down, and it continued operating at the same speed. Once again, I had him turn it down even further with no change in the speed.

The module, identical to the one at Pago Pago, continued to operate fully until he reached the lowest possible power setting, one-click above the "off" setting. At that point, it stopped. It did not slow down; it was either on or off.

It was a complete fabrication by the expert witness. Unfortunately, it shows that you can get experts to testify to anything—right or wrong. In this instance, it set up some of *Perry Mason* Moments. These are moments that are unlikely to ever-present themselves again during my career and likely never present themselves during most lawyer's careers.

The Verdict: "We the Jury…"

The crash of Flight 806 in Pago Pago was, as noted, my first jury trial at the Department of Justice, and as I've already hinted, it was a trial of many firsts for me. Among those was a jury verdict. Remember, this was the culmination of years of work. Keep in mind that plaintiffs are not entitled to juries when they sue the United States for negligence. A judge, not a jury, always decide these trials, and this was the first case I had ever known of that went to a jury. It was a baptism by fire.

After months of trial and years of my life, the Judge gave the jury instructions, and they went off to deliberate. My experience is that juries take their job seriously. They understand that litigants have worked for years on a case before the matter is even presented to them. They have seen and heard the culmination of all that work play out in the courtroom. They want to render a fair decision based on the trial.

In this case, the jury consisted of five women and one man, Michael Brent. Mr. Brent had been chosen to be Jury Foreman, which later proved to lead to a problem. The process took longer than it probably should have because of a lone holdout who insisted that Pan Am was guiltless. She held her ground and was unfazed by arguments from the other jurors. After two days, she finally capitulated and agreed to go along with the others, so on July 27, 1978, they had a verdict.

When word came that the jury had a decision, it was a very tense day as we gathered to hear their verdict. Lawyers worked on this case for years. We had traveled to American Samoa, as well as Hawaii and San Francisco, to take depositions. In Los Angeles, we sat in a magistrate's courtroom, taking depositions week after week over the course of several months. The trial itself was intense with emotional twists and turns. When the jury came into the courtroom with a verdict, the tension was heavy.

What they saw as they entered the courtroom was several lawyers representing the plaintiffs at the counsel table. Boeing had three or four lawyers and a bunch of paralegals and support associates who worked on the case. Several lawyers also represented Pan American. Then there was my colleague who had assisted and me, and that was it for the United States.

The Judge obtained the verdict from the jury, looked at it, and gave it back to the Marshall, who returned it to the Jury Foreman. The Foreman stood to read the verdict and the question.

The first question was, "Do you find the United States was negligent?"

The Foreman replied, "Yes."

"Do you find that that negligence was a proximate cause of the accident?" was the next question on the form.

Once again, the Foreman said, "Yes."

I was crushed; absolutely crushed. I was devastated.

This had been the high point of my life's professional work, and I lost. None of those *Perry Mason* Moments mattered because, at the end of the day, I lost the case. At that time, I took it very personally.

I leaned over to my colleague and told him to call the Department and let them know the outcome. Everyone at Justice knew the decision was coming on that day; certainly, the Civil Division and probably the Assistant Attorney General and perhaps even higher. When my associate left the courtroom to make the call, remember this is an era before cell phones, he had to find a payphone or travel to our office downstairs in the courthouse.

The jury continued to report their findings.

"Was Pan Am negligent?"

"Yes."

"Was that negligence a cause or proximate cause of the accident?"

"Yes."

The jury continued to deliver their verdicts. This was important because of the issue of *willful misconduct*. Under international conventions and limitations printed on each passenger's ticket was a contract. If plaintiffs proved willful misconduct, the amount of damages that can be awarded was much more severe. It becomes an absolute liability or the highest degree of care in exchange for a limit on damages unless there is willful misconduct.

The next question asked was, "Was the conduct of Pan American willful misconduct?"

The jury Foreman answered, "Yes."

I took consolation in this answer. At least the limitation had been lifted because the jury felt that Pan Am had acted willfully in connection with the carriage of extra fuel. They tried to save money by stocking up on cheaper fuel from New Zealand. The extra weight made the already tricky guide slope in Pago Pago more significant. Although I took some consolation in this finding, I was barely listening at that point. I was distracted by internalizing the fact that I had lost the case after all my work.

Next, they moved to the verdicts against Boeing. I don't remember what happened other than there was some confusion. The Judge called counsel to approach the bench to sort out some things. I was only half listening as all the other lawyers went to the sidebar. You've seen it on television when the Judge and lawyers whisper back and forth to one another about an issue they don't want the jury to hear. The next thing I heard was the Jury Foreman. He had sat down from delivering the verdicts when the lawyers went to the bench, but now he stood up, and I could hear his voice.

He said, "Your honor, have you read the verdicts for the United States?"

That obviously caught my attention.

When the Judge answered affirmatively, the Foreman replied, "Your Honor, I believe there's been a mistake."

At that moment, I stood up, probably involuntarily. The Judge looked at me and then at the Foreman, and said, "Sir, we'll get back to that in a second, so please, have a seat."

Both the Foreman and I sat down, and the Judge returned to sorting out the issues with the Boeing claims and sent the lawyers back to their seats. Then he finished reading the Boeing verdict before looking at me as he said, "Mr. Dombroff, I suspect you'd like to approach the bench."

As I answered affirmatively, I literally sprinted to the bench. The other lawyers joined us as we all approached the Judge.

Whispering once again, the Judge said, "I believe he said there might have been an error in the verdict."

"No, your Honor," I replied, "He said there **was** an error in the verdict."

"What I'm going to do is give them the verdict form as to the United States which had been read as the United States was negligent and that negligence was a cause of the accident. I'm going to give the Foreman and the jury the verdict form and send them back to the jury room. I'm not going to do anything else, other than ask them to look at the verdict form and return."

That's precisely what he did as he instructed the Forman and jurors to return to the jury room and take the action they deem appropriate in their discretion. I just sat at the table during those few minutes the jury was gone. After a few minutes, the jury returned, and the entire courtroom was electric.

This was all new to me. I had never experienced anything like this, and remember, this was the first jury trial for me. Once the jury was in place, the Judged asked the Foreman to give the verdict form to the clerk. It was passed to the Judge, and after reading it, handed it back and said, "Sir, please read the verdict as to the United States. Do you find the United States was negligent?"

The answer was, "No," from the Foreman.

The Judge then noted for the record that the jury had crossed out the prior answers of yes for questions one and two about the United States being negligent. They also indicated "no" to question one and initialed it. The other answer to the United States was blank as they had found no negligence.

Initially, the jury unanimously found the United States was not negligent, but in marking the form, the Foreman simply made a mistake. While the lawyers were at the sidebar discussing the Boeing question, several jurors leaned over to the Foreman and whispered to him that he had made a mistake. That's what caused him to stand up and get the Judge's attention.

About the time the corrected verdict was read, my colleague came back into the courtroom. He had called the office. He had sat down next to me, and the court was still in session because the Judge was going through additional comments.

As soon as my colleague sat down, I said, "You're not going to believe this, but go back and call the Department and tell them we won, and that the prior verdict was wrong."

I quickly explained how they marked it wrong, and we won the case. The look on his face was priceless as he got up and went back out to the phone.

When court was adjourned that day, it was the culmination of years of work for me. I went to the Deputy Clerk, who had been in the courtroom the entire trial, and asked if I could have the verdict form. I wanted the one that had the "yes" crossed out. She replied that she couldn't give me the original but offered to run back to the Judge's chambers and make a copy for me. I have that copy of the verdict form hanging on my wall. I have never experienced anything like that since, and frankly, I hope I never will.

Colgan Airways: A Family Affair

Although there are still many people who experience anxiety about getting on a plane, the airline industry in the United States is remarkably safe. In fact, most studies report that air travel is the safest form of transportation. The last catastrophic accident that the airline passenger industry experienced was in 2009, more than a decade ago. Since that time, United States airlines have transported approximately eight billion passengers without a single fatality from a crash.

The crash on February 12, 2009, was a Colgan Airway Q400, a twin-engine turboprop. The flight left Newark, New Jersey, destined for Buffalo, New York. An eyewitness just outside of Buffalo reported hearing the plane sputter, then the engine completely stopped, followed by an explosion. The airplane struck a house, and the ensuing investigation concluded the cause was fundamental piloting errors. Allegedly, both the Captain and the Co-pilot were fatigued, which produced lapses in judgment. When the plane stalled, the pilot reacted opposite of how he should. The airplane system tried to correct the problem, but the pilot's actions as they attempted to save the airplane, essentially overcame the system's attempt at correction.

When the airplane hit a house on a residential street, all 49 souls on board were killed, along with one person who was inside the house. Significant property damage also occurred as a result of the explosion and fire after the crash.

I mention Colgan Airways because I represented them, and had been doing so since early 2003. Colgan was a family-owned company, founded by Senator Charles Colgan, the then most senior senator in the Virginia statehouse. After serving as a military pilot, he founded the predecessor to Colgan that was subsequently sold before he started the second life of Colgan Airways.

They operated as an express carrier for US Airways. All their planes were painted in US Airways colors and had US Airways on the side. Like many airplanes that are express operators for larger carriers, the only way passengers would know is if they read the boarding pass, which typically indicates that the airplane is US Airways Express operated by Colgan Airways.

I began representing Colgan in 2003. The first matter I handled for them was an accident involving a Beech 1900 airplane, substantially smaller and less sophisticated than the Q400. Also, it was less powerful and had fewer seats, only 19 compared to 70.

The Beech 1900 had undergone some maintenance before taking off from Martha's Vineyard. They were enroute to have some black box recorders that recalibrated after the maintenance. Shortly after the plane took off, it nosed into the water off the coast near Hyannis, Massachusetts. Both the pilot and co-pilot were killed. Ultimately, the accident investigation determined that one of the flight control surfaces was rigged or set up incorrectly.

The cables that controlled the flight control surfaces of that airplane ran from the front of the airplane in the cockpit, all the way back to the tail. During the just-completed maintenance, they were rigged incorrectly. Essentially it was done backward. As a result, when the pilots took off and began to climb, although the pilots did it correctly, the faulty cables caused the plane to fly into the ground. They got the opposite results they intended. The fly up command was translated into a fly down movement.

The pilots had no idea of what went wrong. It was at a low altitude with no time to diagnose the problem. There was nothing they could do to keep from crashing into the water. It was a real tragedy.

Colgan, my client, sued Beech, which at that time was owned by Raytheon, for damages with respect to the loss of the aircraft hull. Families of the pilot and co-pilot brought their own actions against Beech. We sued for the monies the insurer had paid to Colgan for the aircraft hull, as well as other money that Colgan had expended as a result of the accident.

The discovery prior to the trial revealed that the maintenance manual published by Beech was the culprit. The work done was depicted backward in the manual. Earlier versions of the manual had the same mistake, and it was surprising another operator had never picked it up. It was sort of a head-scratcher as to why there had not been a previous accident caused by a backward system. Perhaps it was a maintenance procedure that was not done frequently on airplanes.

The check to make sure the plane functioned properly was also confusing. It relied on one mechanic in the cockpit and one on the scaffolding in the back of the plane, looking up. They shouted "up" or "down" to one another as they checked the system. The manual was not clear about what "up" or "down" specified. Did it mean the control surface was moving "up" or moving "down," or was the airplane supposed to be flying "up" or "down" or the pedals? The whole thing was confusing.

The day before we were scheduled to go to trial, the judge, Albert Bryan, Jr. in the Eastern District of Virginia in Alexandria, Virginia, gave a whole series of adverse rulings on various evidentiary motions. The judge issued his rulings based on Virginia law that he was familiar with, but I argued that Massachusetts law is what applied to this case. We contended that Colgan simply needed to prove that the manual was defective, which it was and that under Massachusetts law, it was not a defense to Raytheon that the mechanics or pilots may have been negligent. The night before we were to pick the jury, the judge instructed me to write a jury instruction that conformed to what we felt was an erroneous ruling with respect to jury instruction. I remember vividly telling the judge that I couldn't do that. My reasoning was because the law in Massachusetts didn't support it. With a wave of a hand, he dismissed my protestations and said he'd see me at nine o'clock in the morning.

The next morning when the judge entered the courtroom, he took the bench, and I remember his words addressed to the counsel. "Counsel, we've hit a speed bump overnight. I have looked at the positions that Mr. Drombroff argued yesterday, and I believe he's correct."

All the lawyers, for Raytheon, my colleague, and I, were stunned. I was particularly surprised because I had tried other cases before Judge Bryan, and I never anticipated he would reverse himself. He added that in light of that fact, he went back and reversed his rulings on all the motions on behalf of my client, he had overruled. After that, he called for a 15-minute recess and added, "I suspect counsel might want to confer among themselves."

During that recess, the lawyer for Raytheon indicated he wanted to go back to his clients and talk to them. That night, he called me and offered one hundred percent of our damages, everything we had sued for. The next morning, we reported to the judge the case had been settled. He probably knew that would happen once he reversed his earlier rulings. He knew that even if the Colgan mechanics or pilots were negligent, under Massachusetts law, that would not be a defense for Raytheon to strict product liability and a defective manual. Since the manual was defective, any contributory negligence, even if proven, would not be a defense.

I bring up my work with Colgan because of another case that occurred in 2007. The case was Khan vs. Colgan Airways, and it turned out to be one of the most memorable cases I ever had. The case arose out of the termination of a co-pilot named Rao Zahid Khan, a young pilot of Pakistani descent. I mention this because it comes into play later in this case. He was based in West Virginia, and like all the pilots and co-pilots, was required to undergo annual training and checks. The requirements for co-pilots were less strenuous than for pilots, but Mr. Khan still had a frequent test. Testing was conducted in the airplane, and he sat in the right seat, the co-pilot's seat. Also in the cockpit was the chief pilot and the check airman, who was responsible for evaluating Mr. Kahn. The options were pass or fail to perform maneuvers properly. After the first maneuver fails, the check stops, and retraining is provided on the spot. At that point, they resume the check. Under FAA rules, this can be done two times during a check.

It happened twice with Mr. Khan. After it happened the third time, and the check airman and chief pilot had to intervene because they were concerned for their own safety. They took control of the airplane, terminated the check, and failed Mr. Khan.

At that time, Colgan did not have the money to send Mr. Khan back to training. They would also have to take him offline as a pilot because he couldn't even fly as a co-pilot until he completed expensive simulator training. Post 9/11, Colgan had come close to bankruptcy and was forced to cut back any unnecessary expenses. Since he couldn't fly and they couldn't afford to train him, coupled with the air safety considerations, Mr. Khan was terminated.

In a short time, Mr. Kahn filed a complaint with the West Virginia Human Rights Commission. Colgan had a crew in West Virginia, so that's why they had jurisdiction in his case. He asserted that he had been discriminated against based on events from one or two years earlier. In fact, he had been the subject of some horrific treatment by other pilots. The misconduct of two pilots occurred at the West Virginia crew base. They wrote disparaging comments on his locker. However, Colgan acted properly at the time, giving warnings and advised if they did it again, they would be terminated.

Time went by, and then Mr. Khan failed his proficiency check. Now he is asserting that his termination was not in connection with air safety or any other valid reason. Instead, he claimed it was retaliation for the earlier events with the other pilots. The complaint was filed with the filing of the complaint with the Human Rights Commission.

On behalf of Colgan, I filed a response denying Mr. Kahn's accusation, pointing out that it was a matter of air safety. Our firm had local counsel in West Virginia, and they made it a point to tell me that 98% of all complaints filed in front of the Human Rights Commission are decided in favor of the employee. In this case, if accurate, that would mean they would find in favor of Mr. Khan. There was no way Calgon was going to settle the matter, so they instructed us to proceed.

We went to a hearing that took place at the West Office of the West Virginia Human Rights Commission. As I recall, it was a partially deserted shopping mall with an unusual configuration of cubicles, many of which had walls that didn't reach the ceiling. We were in one of the closed rooms, and the hearing lasted two or three days. I was impressed with the Hearing Examiner as he paid attention and asked decent questions. We had the check airman and chief pilot testify, and I thought the hearing went well. Our local counsel, who was present throughout the hearing, shared my optimism based on the historical performance of these types of proceedings.

Our optimism was rewarded, and we won. The hearing examiner wrote an opinion finding that the discharge of Mr. Khan was not discriminatory. Obviously, we were pleased because we believed it was the correct result, but like all matters in litigation, administrative or otherwise, the plaintiff has the right to appeal to the members of the commission itself, which he exercised. The Human Rights Commission reversed the hearing examiner and found that we had acted in a discriminatory manner. We were ordered to reinstate him. The simple matter of fact is there was no way Calgon was reinstating him as a pilot.

We appealed once again, but this time the appeal went to the West Virginia Supreme Court. It was discretionary with the court whether to accept our appeal, and we were pleased when they did. In mind, it was a good signal that the Supreme Court was concerned about what happened. If all they intended to do was rubber-stamp the Human Rights Commission, they didn't need to accept the appeal. We had hope.

The case involving Mr. Khan became very interesting once the Supreme Court of West Virginia accepted the appeal. We had the opportunity to file briefs. Since the Human Rights Commission reversed the hearing examiner and found in favor of Mr. Khan, we were now the losing party. That meant this case became Colgan Air Inc. vs. West Virginia Human Rights Commission. The State Attorney General was involved in defending the Human Rights Commission. We filed our brief, and they filed their reply brief, which said we were wrong and that the discharge was discriminatory and retaliatory.

The lawyer working with me on this case from the beginning had worked on several Colgan matters unrelated to this case. She was a very competent attorney who spent hundreds of hours working on this case from the time the claim was first made. It happened that she was Pakistani. She was, and is, a bright lawyer. Don't forget, Mr. Khan was also Pakistani. The case began with accusations that Mr. Khan was harassed by the aforementioned pilots because of his ethnicity about a year before his failed flight check. My colleague worked with me from the beginning of this case, as well as previously many other Calgon matters.

Out of nowhere one day, we received a notice in the mail from the West Virginia Supreme Court. It advised they were holding a special Supreme Court session at the theater at Marshall University in Huntington, West Virginia. The theater was large and made it possible for many high school and college students to view firsthand how the Supreme Court worked. Five cases, including ours, were chosen to be heard on that day, so the students would have the opportunity to hear a variety of arguments. It included five different cases representing five areas of the law.

The cases were scheduled for the morning and afternoon, with a luncheon sponsored by the West Virginia Bar Association for the Supreme Court in between. The luncheon was in a nearby building and also served as a time to honor members of the Supreme Court. It was a big occasion. Students from across the state were there to observe.

Our case was scheduled for the morning, the last one before lunch. I remember sitting in a large theater, many times larger than the spectator section of any courtroom anywhere. The proceedings were impressive. The room was full. The Supreme Court Justices sat on a dais on the stage. Flowers were spread across the entire width of their bench, and arguments by the lawyers were made from a lectern in front of the bench. The bench was long enough for all of the judges to sit *en banc*. It was a remarkable sight.

I had previously argued before appellate courts all over the United States, and several state Supreme Courts. I had appeared, not argued before the U.S. Supreme Court, but this was a memorable experience. I presented my argument, and as I went through the case, there were numerous questions. Chief

Justice Robin Davis, a woman, asked several questions. The Attorney from the Attorney General's office argued on behalf of the Human Rights Commission.

My emphasis throughout this case was the issue of aviation safety and the claim that years after Mr. Khan's conflict with the other pilots, the company retaliated was nonsensical. Calgon's actions were all about safety. The fact that the chief pilot had to step in and take over control of the plane was because of fear for his own safety. The company did not have the money to send this co-pilot back for more training because of its continuing financial struggles. There was nothing retaliatory or discriminatory in their actions.

The Attorney General's office argued the contrary, and when I made my rebuttal, I was questioned by Justice Starcher.

He asked, "I couldn't help but notice that you had a colleague, another attorney on this matter with you, Ms. Shaleeza Altaf."

I replied, "Yes, your honor, Ms. Altaf is seated to my right."

"By chance, is she Pakistani or of Pakistani descent?" the judge replied.

I was taken aback and not sure how to respond. It was a shocking question. The question had no relationship to anything I had said. I simply responded, "She is your honor."

He had been holding a pencil, something like a number two yellow pencil, and he leaned back in his chair and threw the pencil onto the table in front of him, and almost disgustedly said, "I thought so."

I heard the gasping; maybe I felt the sound of shock ripple throughout the theater behind me. Frankly, I was appalled.

As I sat down, My colleague got up and calmly walked to the rear of the theater and out the back doors. I can't even begin to imagine how she felt to be singled out for her ethnicity by a State Supreme Court Justice in front of hundreds of people.

When I looked up at the Justices, the Chief Justice had a look of despair on her face and mouthed the words to me, "I'm sorry." I think she and all the other justices were as appalled as I was.

The court adjourned for lunch, so I left to find my colleague, who was clearly upset. It seemed clear that Justice Starcher was dismissing her in this case involving a co-pilot of Pakistani descent.

When I went outside, I noticed she was surrounded by numerous members of the West Virginia Bar Association who were there for the luncheon. It was obvious as I got close that she was upset. They were apologizing on behalf of the Bar Association, trying to provide comfort. I walked over and got her, and we began walking toward the parking lot to make the drive back to Washington.

Our path carried us back inside on the way to the other side of the building and the parking lot. As we walked through the building, we saw the Chief Justice accompanied by one of the Marshals. They were headed to the luncheon, and a glass wall separated us. When she reached the door, as she pushed it open, she stopped and made a gesture beckoning Shaleeza to join her.

I watched as the Chief Justice put her arm around her. It was clear at the time, and I confirmed it later, the Chief Justice was apologizing on behalf of the court. On our road trip back to Washington, we talked about the experience. Back at the office,

I had already received at least 50 communications from members of the West Virginia Bar apologizing for what had happened. With that kind of support, we decided to file a motion to disqualify Justice Starcher from sitting on this case and participating in the decision-making process.

In West Virginia, as in most states, there are essentially no appeals from the Supreme Court, except to the U.S. Supreme Court. Justice Starcher wrote a decision denying our motion to disqualify him, basically accusing me of using my colleague as a prop to neutralize the fact that Mr. Kahn was of Pakistani descent, suggesting we were trying to neutralize the ethnicity issue by her presence.

When Calgon read what the Justice wrote, they were incensed. We filed another motion based on his order, again moving to disqualify him, expressing our outrage. Once again, he denied our motion, but he did it this time in one or two short sentences, with no characterizations. The whole episode was mind-boggling.

The rest of the story is that the West Virginia Supreme Court reversed the Human Rights Commission, reinstated the hearing examiner's decision regarding retaliation and discrimination. Their decision agreed with our contention that Mr. Khan's termination was based on aviation safety and other non-actionable matters, including the inability to have the money to pay for additional training.

We won the case. It was a remarkable experience, one that I hope not ever to repeat or that my colleagues will ever have to endure.

Fifty Years of Lessons

Ancient Greek philosopher Plato, quoting his teacher Socrates, affirmed that "the unexamined life is not worth living." That's kind of what I'm doing with this book, examining my life. Anytime you examine your life, there is much to be learned. As I look at my professional career and the various cases and experiences along the way, a number of important lessons come to the forefront. Hopefully, these lessons can provide assistance and encouragement as you pursue your life goals.

Lesson One: Everybody should be a magician.

I don't mean that you should run out to your local magic store even assuming you could find one anywhere except on the Internet, or that you force your kids to take up magic as a hobby. What I mean is to encourage your children to do something that gets them in front of people as early as you can.

In my case, it was magic. I didn't think of it like that when I was six or seven; it was something for me to do. I didn't even realize I was annoying the heck out of my parents and grandparents, friends, and everyone else I could get to stand still long enough for me to do a trick.

There is a wide range of activities and hobbies that encourage children to be in front of a group. It might be a local theater group, singing, playing an instrument. Many take up something early in life as a child; others have waited until later in life. Your age doesn't matter. Pick a hobby that will put you in front of people and talking to them. Such a skill will bridge gaps between people and build your confidence. If you do become a lawyer or your child chooses it for their future, it's a skill that will serve you the rest of your life.

In my case, I certainly didn't set out to choose magic as a hobby, so I would be comfortable in the courtroom, speaking before large groups, or appearing on television. That wasn't my intent, but it was a direct result of speaking and performing in front of people since I was six or seven-years-old. It has never been a source of fear for me. If you were to ask my parents, they would tell you that I drove them crazy, but they've seen that it's an invaluable skill to have in life.

Lessons 2: You should always assume that every matter you handle as a lawyer is going to trial.

Obviously, a trial is not the desired endgame of most legal matters, but complete preparation is equally applicable to every kind of issue in life. Lawyers handle many cases that never go to trial, or even needed to go to trial. It's very expensive. It's risky. Frankly, I've never met a client who wants a case to go to trial. Juries are unpredictable, and nobody wants to face such great uncertainty.

However, from a lawyer's perspective, it's beneficial to assume from day one that the matter you're handling is going to trial. What I mean is that everything you do from the beginning needs to be calculated toward preparing for the courtroom or whatever the endgame. Ironically, taking this approach means that a case will be far more likely to end with a settlement or resolution, other than a trial.

I've had a few clients over the years who consciously decide they don't want the matter handled in any other way than focused toward a settlement. My only caution with every contact with the client is to remind them that the best way to signal that you intend to settle is to not prepare for trial. It's never in your best interest to make it clear from day one that you will compromise. I learned this as a young lawyer, and it's no less true today with many things in life.

Lesson 3: Hire astronauts and generals.

I described several cases I handed over the years that taught me a great deal about expert witnesses. Particularly, Flight 405 in Cleveland, Flight 1016 in Charlotte, and Flight 427 in Pittsburgh. In each, my expert was either an astronaut or a general, or both.

The lesson I took away from those cases and discussions with lawyers and jurors after each trial was the power of an expert witness. In my cases, there is no substitute for astronauts or generals. What this says is that if you want a superstar type expert, locate that individual who is not only highly qualified in their area but also one who brings a "wow" factor into the courtroom. That person is difficult to cross-examine, and it's nearly impossible for the other side to create credibility problems.

This approach worked out frequently throughout my career, and I am diligent today in terms of hiring witnesses to speak for my client. It doesn't mean they are all astronauts and generals. It might involve witnesses whose names are readily known to the jurors, but it might also be someone who comes from a high leadership position in industry or government. The fact that they occupy their position gives them layers of credibility and makes their testimony and their credibility essentially bulletproof.

Lessons 4: It's not your case.

As a lawyer, you are representing a client. Even though we might colloquially refer to a case that we're handling as "my case," you always have to remember that it's not your case. It's always the client's case. This is not a distinction without a difference. No matter what you as an individual, either profes-

Arguing before the Washington State Supreme Court

sionally or personally, want to do concerning the case, at the end of the day, it's the client's case, and it's their agenda which matters...not yours.

It is certainly appropriate to offer your opinion and even try to persuade the client to see it your way, but it's never your case. It's your job to keep the client fully informed concerning upsides and downsides, along with risks and benefits. In the end, it's their decision as to what to do, not yours.

Lesson 5: Always respond immediately.

Email is not a substitute for snail mail; it's completely wiped regular mail service off the table. In my mind, there's a sense of urgency to email. It doesn't take days to arrive at the destination, just seconds, and it should not take days, or even hours, for a response.

My practice is to check my email frequently, which means, in my case, I'm obsessively on my phone in order to respond immediately. That response might simply be an acknowledgment their email was received, and I'm aware of their need. Sometimes nothing more than "I'm on it," or "I'll get back to you promptly." It's an immediate response. Almost always, I will respond within a few minutes.

The goal is to provide them with the comfort of knowing their concern will be handled. When people wait one or two days for a response, they will spend much of that time wondering if their communication was received and heard. There is never an excuse for not responding or acknowledging an email.

Lesson 6: Never assume that what you're hearing is correct.

Early in my career, I learned this valuable lesson during one of the most interesting cases. It was the Pan Am crash in Pago Pago featuring the testimony of Mr. Frampton (see Chapter "*Perry Mason* Moment: Pago Pago"). As I related, he spoke of something called *reverse sensing* that he saw on the flight check recordings. The easiest course would have been to conclude that this highly experienced expert knew what he was talking about.

However, my expert, Richard McFarland, was sitting next to me at the table, and I immediately determined that what I was hearing was incorrect. As unlikely as it seemed, it wasn't an issue of spin or interpretation or difference of opinion; it was flat out wrong.

When you hear things from witnesses (your own or for the other side) or lawyers (your own colleagues or the other side), consider what you are hearing, or for that matter, anyone. This means to not only think about the context but also if the information you are hearing is correct. It's far too easy for people, even without knowing it, to say things that are wrong, either out of ignorance or intentionally. Don't assume that what you hear is accurate and correct.

Lesson 7: Always prove who committed the murder.

Since I cut my legal teeth watching Raymond Burr as *Perry Mason*, I was accustomed to a full 60 minutes that included the commission of a crime, the perpetrator arrested, Mason investigating, assisted by Paul Drake and Della Street, and a trial. Inevitably, at some point in the trial, Perry not only demonstrated that his client was innocent but also unveiled the true murderer who was predictably sitting in the courtroom.

This process was effective for dramatic television. It also conditioned viewers, and in this case, generations of viewers, to expect the same thing in real life. Jurors expect something similar. Lawyers should be prepared to demonstrate not only the innocence of their client but also provide an alternative theory or perpetrator.

No matter what kind of case you're handling, even though you don't have a legal burden to identify the real guilty party or wrongdoers, remember that jurors want answers. They want to know the responsible party for committing the crime or causing an injury. The standards of the law don't require an attorney to prove innocence by providing an alternative explanation but supplying such information will go a long way toward allowing the jury to let your client off.

From the beginning, plan to demonstrate what happened according to an alternative theory beyond the fact that your client didn't do anything wrong.

Lesson 8: Write and speak and then write and speak more.

In today's world of social media and Internet access to information, there is no excuse for any lawyer not having a public profile. It can be *Twitter*, *Facebook*, writing a blog, or numerous other avenues, but you can use your online presence to elevate your profile in ways that were not available just a few years ago.

When I started my legal career, there were various law reviews, and legal publications printed on paper and sent to subscribers or association members. Today, everybody is a publisher. A distribution network is available to anyone who chooses. That means you should be writing, speaking, and doing webinars.

This allows you to become recognized as an expert in your field. You will also discover that a high-level profile ultimately contributes to business development. One of the first things people do before entering a business relationship or seeking a

lawyer is to turn to the Internet. It doesn't require a computer genius to discover a person's profile. In fact, you want people to find your profile easily.

Write and speak and do it with as much frequency as you can possibly accomplish.

Lesson 9: You'll never be fully prepared.

I don't recall a single case where I felt fully prepared on the day of the trial and that there was nothing left to do. Since my experience covers five decades, that's an extraordinary statement. The fact is that you can never be too prepared. It becomes even more complicated as the case drags on. Every continuance uncovers additional preparation that is necessary, so having more time should not result in you concluding you're fully prepared. There's always more that can be done. Refine your opening statement. Review your direct and cross-examinations, and so forth.

Every time I stood to make an opening statement to the jury or argue a motion to a judge, I have always felt I could have prepared even more. The fact is that you can always prepare more.

Lessons 10: Never be reluctant to try a new approach.

Experience has taught me that it always pays off to think outside the box. It doesn't necessarily mean that the thinking turns into action. Recognizing that innovative thoughts and approaches can provide a significant payoff means you should not be quick to dismiss something new and different.

An example is the approach I took with several lawsuits described in earlier chapters when I told the jury during the opening statement that my client was at fault for negligence. I quickly added, though, there was no conduct to be punished. This admission took the sting out of arguments made by the other side and eliminated any emotionally driven punishment of my client. By virtue of admitting our failure, we removed the jury's need to make a statement that we had failed.

In each instance, this approach was discussed extensively with the client prior to the trial. In many respects, it was a foreign approach—admitting liability for negligence during a liability trail doesn't make sense to some. However, it allowed us to argue successfully that punitive liability was unnecessary and unwarranted.

Perhaps an even more effective approach that was considered non-traditional was the way we handled arguing damages. In a damages trial, during the opening statement, I told the jury how much they should award and explained that the evidence would prove the amount we suggested was an appropriate amount.

Beforehand, I described to the clients that it would give the jury a frame of reference to consider when it came to awarding damages. We didn't want to leave them with whatever number they could pull out of the air. It also told the jury to make sure the plaintiff wasn't asking for more than the evidence suggested as appropriate. I provided them a guideline for making their decision.

Jurys are often selected because of their complete lack of knowledge. More often than not, this is the first time they have been on a jury. Suddenly, they are asked to *spend* someone else's money, and frequently in amounts beyond their own life experience. By giving the jury a number that I thought was appropriate and established by the evidence, it provided a point of reference. As I look over my cases, both in terms of liability and damage awards, the cases where I suggested an amount, the approach clearly paid off.

Punitive damages or punitive conduct was not awarded in any of these cases. There was nothing to punish. In every instance in which the jury was asked to award compensatory damages, not punitive, and the jury awarded an amount equal to or actually even less than the amount I had suggested.

The bottom line is always to think outside the box. Look for a different way to do something and never be afraid to proceed. Obviously, if you need the approval of a client, then get it, but don't let that stop you from considering and discussing innovative approaches.

Lesson 11: The best defense is a good offense.

There is nothing original about this concept but applying it to the practice of law is a good approach to keep in mind. I've discussed it within the context of *Perry Mason*, always proving not only the innocence of his client but also the identity of the wrongdoer. If you are representing defendants in a case, your approach should take into consideration that the best defense is a good offense. Don't wait until the plaintiff attacks before you respond. Move the case forward. Communicate the message that your client is ready, willing, and able to go to trial and raise the stakes. Don't be totally reactive.

Lesson 12: Marketing versus Business Development

Over the course of my career, I have spoken to thousands of lawyers at hundreds of legal groups, bar associations, and continuing legal education programs. Out of all those opportunities, I can only think of one new client that I acquired as a direct result of those speaking engagements to lawyers. The one exception was a lawyer who was in an audience in Wilmington, Delaware. He worked as in-house counsel for a corporation that came to us for representation for several years. There might have been a few other referrals, but I can't think of any.

There is a difference between business development and marketing. As a general rule, speaking to lawyers or attending legal programs doesn't bring any business. It might raise your profile, which is good, and it might also lead to additional speaking engagements, but that's not enough. Speaking only to lawyers can be a good thing, but it is essentially marketing or public relations instead of going out and asking for business.

Willie Sutton was an infamous criminal from the first half of the 20th century. He was especially known for robbing banks. He has been credited for responding to a reporter's question of why he robbed banks by saying, "That's where the money is." It became known as *Sutton's Law*, even though he denied ever making the comment.

We might not know who made this statement first, but it is something of a guideline as to how lawyers should operate. Many think the best way to build a law practice is to develop relationships with lawyers. As I discovered, that's not an effective approach. I try to limit my speaking engagements and activities to where clients can be found—industry trade associations, client groups, general counsel, etc., essentially with people who give out business.

This realization explains why I started the *Aviation Symposium* 15 years ago and don't allow outside lawyers to attend. In the room are 500 clients or prospective clients and my team, no one else. It's like digging a gigantic hole, filling it with water and fish, and having the only boat. We're the only ones allowed to fish.

Business development for lawyers is no different than business development for any other business. Speaking before lawyers and good marketing and public relations are good for building a profile, but they are not substitutes for speaking to potential clients and asking for their business.

Lesson 13: Innovate, Invent, and Create

As a general rule, I think most lawyers are lousy businessmen. This is my observation after practicing law for 50 years. Partners in law firms, no matter how experienced they are or how good they are at the law, don't know how to ask for business. They often feel it's beneath them. They're not motivated to ask for business because they have never had to build a practice. Out of law school, they joined a firm, became an associate, and worked for a partner who inherited clients from another partner. These clients had become institutionalized, so the lawyer was not required to build the practice. I have lawyers I've worked with who have never built a practice.

I never had that benefit. Nobody ever handed off clients to me. At Hughes Hubbard & Reed, I was not handed any clients. They hired me right from the government and expected me to build the aviation part of the business myself. The wonderful thing about working for the DOJ was that the FAA was my captive client. However, in private practice, I had to build my practice with no guarantees. All I had was my self-confidence and legal credentials.

One of the things I did, even before entering private practice, was to attend a large aviation law conference in Dallas and started hosting a private dinner on the night of the conference banquet. Typically, people don't want to go to banquets, so I would normally invite 50 people to a different hotel about ten minutes away. I provided small busses for transportation and small gift bags, and I always did a magic show. I don't think there's anyone in my client or prospect base who doesn't know about my magic, and that sets me apart from every other lawyer. That's important.

This ultimately led to the *Aviation Symposium* that we do every year. The Symposium came about after I attended an educational program held at the National Transportation Safety Board; they investigate all transportation accidents, the sole authority for such things. I attended a course at their academy in 2006. The aviation industry has been safe for so long that the last major catastrophic accident involving a passenger airline in this country was 2009, Colgan Airways in Buffalo, New York.

The result of this level of safety was that there was a complete lack of "hands-on" experience within companies that dealt

The Aviation Symposium

with aircraft accidents. Most companies didn't have anyone who had *been there* and *done that*. They all had annual emergency response drills and training, which were essentially "check the box" exercises, so I went to the NTSB academy to see what they offered and concluded I would offer my own program.

Our first Symposium was in 2007, and that first year, I anticipated 20 people. The plan was for a one-day conference held in the conference room of Dombroff & Gilmore. We would tell them what really happens after an accident, and we called it, *An airplane is down…What Really Happens After an Accident!* We wanted them to know what happens, not what a checklist in a book suggests.

The first year, 40 people showed up, and we couldn't fit in the conference room. It has continually grown. Our last conference, one of the last major events before the Covid Virus shut everything down, was at the Ritz Carlton in McLean, Virginia, with over 500 in attendance.

The typical schedule begins with a Tuesday welcome cocktail party and ends with the final session on Thursday morning. We provide all the meals and charge nothing for the food or the conference. On Tuesday night, I host a private dinner for about 30 people, and I always do magic for them. Our Symposium has a reputation among many as being the premier aviation industry event of the year. It is attended by representatives from all the airline manufacturers, insurers, and brokers.

Our 2021 will be the 15th year. We were the last big aviation event of its type in 2020 before the pandemic and the lockdown, and I think we'll be the first once things are loosened up. The Symposium is the ultimate marketing and business development event. Rather than me and another lawyer going out to see a client, we bring 500 clients and prospective clients to us.

We feed people, and we don't charge anything. It has become an annual event for the entire industry, and other meetings are scheduled around our meeting. All aviation-related agencies in the U.S. government are involved. It's the ultimate event!

Connected with the Symposium, we have the *Aviation Symposium Webinar Series*. We hold these webinars between the annual Symposia to keep in touch and keep our name in front of clients. We use social media extensively, especially *LinkedIn* and *Twitter*.

Currently, I have nearly 5,000 *LinkedIn* connections, and that's a carefully curated list built over years. With the recent changes caused by the pandemic, we shifted our business development activities to social media and increased the scope. Currently, we don't have virtual happy hours; we have virtual lunches. In the words of Jerry Seinfeld, our agenda is "Nothing." In other words, we have lunch with our clients, maybe three or four of us and three or four of them. Moreover, we send them an account number so they can order lunch from *Door Dash* or *Uber Eats* on us. Everyone thoroughly enjoys them, and it's something that is going to continue as a regular part of our business development techniques. Plus, I do magic!

During the pandemic lockdown, we have weekly aviation team meetings. During these meetings, we don't talk about cases or law. We discuss developing business, and we invite a client or prospective client to every meeting to talk about their concerns and issues. In addition, we have an annual *Aviation Practice Retreat*, a one-day meeting. Five or six general counsel or insurance company claims executives participate in a moderated panel discussion with our lawyers. They discuss what they like and don't like about outside counsel. They talk about why they hire them, why they fire them, and how they can be helped by them. This is also a business development technique.

What I basically learned from the event in Dallas, which I attended, is don't invite lawyers. At that event, about 90% of the people there were lawyers and only a small number of clients or companies that hired lawyers. Essentially, it was lawyers *circling* the room trolling for business. I saw no point in that, so I decided to have my own Symposium, and we would be the only lawyers in attendance. We don't accept sponsorships, and we don't charge anyone. We pay for everything ourselves. It has turned into the event to attend if you're in the aviation industry.

The other thing I did was create an organization called the *Aviation Emergency Response Organization* (AERO). It is an educational resource association for all phases of emergency response, not only for aviation but also for the cruise industry and other industries involved. It is open to anyone involved in emergency response. AERO has taken on a life of its own. There is now a Board of Directors and a website (aviationemergency. org). Not only is it an emergency responder community, but it is also a development tool for me. I sit on the Board and act as counsel for the organization.

So, innovate, invent, and create! Maybe your business development efforts won't be the same as mine but figure out what works for you and go for it. Remember, there's a big difference between marketing and business development.

Use your imagination!

A Final Word: My Magic Life

Over the years, I've come to realize that adults, as opposed to children, are the easiest to fool with magic. Children live in the moment and enjoy what they see in front of them. Adults think logically and tend to think to the end of the trick, anticipating what the magician will do. So when the outcome is not logical, adults are fooled. When working at the Justice Department, I was a birthday magician and loved entertaining the kids because all you need to do is fool them. With adults, the result has to be something that is not logical; an ending they have not thought of themselves. It's important to catch them off guard with a twist that's not the expected, logical conclusion to the trick.

In many ways, my life has experienced a great deal of magic. I don't mean simple trickery designed to fool innocent children. I'm speaking of the kind of magic best appreciated by unsuspecting adults who think they already know what the trick will be. The end is a surprise, something completely unexpected. Many of the stories I have related in the preceding chapters took you to places that were not anticipated.

Who would have thought a young boy, born to parents who were both lawyers and raised in an environment that pointed to a legal career, would be captivated by a few simple magic tricks that he learned as a child and followed a legal career that was also filled with magical occurrences.

I've defined "*Perry Mason* Moments" for you, things that most lawyers never experience. It's not an exaggeration to say that each time, as I watched these moments unfold in the courtroom, it was magic. There's an amazing moment when I realize what is about to happen, and that's a better feeling than any magic trick has ever provided.

Magic is also a good word to describe the people I've met along the way. Not just met these people but became good friends with many. The list includes astronauts, famous generals, courtroom wizards, legal geniuses, famous judges, media personalities, and well-respected politicians. They have been peppered through my career like magic dust.

Many others have brought magic to my life because they put their trust in me to help them through a difficult situation. I think of clients who faced the unknown. Airplane crashes always impact numerous lives, and I have had the opportunity to help bring closure to an unexplainable tragedy. The only trick to that process is hard work.

The magic collection at my house continues to grow as I discover new tricks. I also anticipate that my magic life will continue to experience many amazing opportunities, both in the courtroom and on the performance stage.

www.ingramcontent.com/pod-product-compliance
Lightning Source LLC
Chambersburg PA
CBHW060534210326

41519CB00014B/3220